*Routledge Revivals*

# The Origin of our Knowledge of Right and Wrong

First published in 1889 and appearing in English in 1969, this title had an extraordinary influence in the field of philosophy. It provided the basis for the theory of value as this was developed by Meinong, Husserl and Scheler. In addition, the doctrine of intentionality that is presented here is central to contemporary philosophy of mind.

# The Origin of our Knowledge of Right and Wrong

Franz Brentano

Edited by Oskar Kraus

English Edition edited by Roderick M. Chisholm

Translated by Roderick M. Chisholm and Elizabeth H. Schneewind

First published in 1889
by Duncker and Humblot, Leipzig
Second edition published in 1921
by Felix Meiner, Leipzig
Third revised edition published in 1934
by Felix Meiner, Leipzig
First published in 1969
by Routledge & Kegan Paul Ltd

This edition first published in 2009 by Routledge
2 Park Square, Milton Park, Abingdon, Oxon, OX14 4RN

Simultaneously published in the USA and Canada
by Routledge
270 Madison Avenue, New York, NY 10016

*Routledge is an imprint of the Taylor & Francis Group, an informa business*
This translation in English © 1969 Routledge & Kegan Paul Ltd

**Publisher's Note**
The publisher has gone to great lengths to ensure the quality of this reprint but
points out that some imperfections in the original copies may be apparent.

**Disclaimer**
The publisher has made every effort to trace copyright holders and welcomes
correspondence from those they have been unable to contact.

ISBN 13: 978-0-415-55739-9 (hbk)
ISBN 13: 978-0-415-55790-0 (pbk)
ISBN 13: 978-0-203-09224-8 (ebk)

ISBN 10: 0-415-55739-9 (hbk)
ISBN 10: 0-415-55790-9 (pbk)
ISBN 10: 0-203-09224-4 (ebk)

# THE ORIGIN OF OUR KNOWLEDGE
## OF RIGHT AND WRONG

# International Library of Philosophy and Scientific Method

*Editor:* Ted Honderich

A Catalogue of books already published in the
*International Library of Philosophy and Scientific Method*
will be found at the end of this volume

# FRANZ BRENTANO

## *The Origin of our Knowledge of Right and Wrong*

---

EDITED BY OSKAR KRAUS

ENGLISH EDITION EDITED BY
RODERICK M. CHISHOLM

*Translated by Roderick M. Chisholm
and Elizabeth H. Schneewind*

ROUTLEDGE & KEGAN PAUL
LONDON AND HENLEY
NEW YORK: HUMANITIES PRESS

*Originally published in 1889*
*by Duncker and Humblot, Leipzig as*
Vom Ursprung sittlicher Erkenntnis

*Second edition published*
*by Felix Meiner, Leipzig 1921*
*Third revised edition published*
*by Felix Meiner 1934*

*First published in 1969*
*by Routledge and Kegan Paul Ltd*
*39 Store Street*
*London WC1E 7DD and*
*Broadway House, Newtown Road*
*Henley-on-Thames*
*Oxon RG9 1EN*

*Printed in Great Britain by*
*Redwood Burn Limited*
*Trowbridge & Esher*

*ISBN 0 7100 6321 0*

# Contents

                                                              page
PREFACE TO THE ENGLISH EDITION                                 vii

AUTHOR'S PREFACE                                                ix

THE LECTURE: The Origin of Our Knowledge of Right and
  Wrong                                                          3

SUPPLEMENTARY NOTES                                             47
  *On Kant's Categorical Imperative*                            49
  *Descartes' Classification of Psychological Phenomena*        50
  *In Defence of a Theory of Judgement*                         54
  *On Existential and Negative Judgements*                      59
  *On the Concepts of Truth and Existence*                      73
  *On the Unity of the Concept of the Good*                     75
  *On the Evident*                                              76
  *Ethical Subjectivism*                                        84
  *Two Unique Cases of Preferability*                           90
  *On the Charge of Excessive Rigorism*                         92
  *Criticism of Ihering*                                        93
  *Mill's Conception of the Evident*                            96
  *Miklosich on Subjectless Propositions*                       98

APPENDICES
    I. *Ethical Principles as A Priori*                        111
   II. *Decisions within the Sphere of the Emotions and the
        Formulation of the Supreme Ethical Commandment*        113
  III. *The Relativity of Secondary Moral Laws*                116
   IV. *Punishment and its Justification*                      118

v

CONTENTS

v. *Epicurus and the War*    122

vi. *The Young Benjamin Franklin's Attack upon Ethics*    125

vii. *On the Moral Perfection of the First Cause of all Contingent Beings*    130

viii. *Happiness and Unhappiness*    134

ix. *Loving and Hating*    137

INTRODUCTION to the 1934 edition by Oskar Kraus    161

INDEX    169

# Preface to the English Edition

The first edition of Franz Brentano's *Vom Ursprung sittlicher Erkenntnis* was published in 1889 by Duncker & Humblot in Leipzig. This was translated by Cecil Hague and published in 1902 by Archibald Constable & Co., Ltd., in London. A second edition, edited by Oskar Kraus, was published by Felix Meiner in Leipzig in 1921. This edition contained as Appendices nine supplementary essays from Brentano's *Nachlass*, as well as an Introduction and explanatory notes by Kraus. A third revised edition, edited by Kraus, was published by Felix Meiner in 1934.

The present translation is a translation of Kraus's third edition. It differs from Kraus's edition in the following respects. It includes everything that Brentano had included in his first edition (Kraus had omitted the essay, "Miklosich on Subjectless Propositions," since this was included in the second edition of Brentano's *Psychologie vom empirischen Standpunkt*, published by Felix Meiner in 1925). Some of Kraus's notes and parts of the Introduction have been abbreviated, some of the notes have been omitted, and references have been brought up to date. I have added a few brief notes; these have my initials.

Two works that had not appeared when Kraus wrote his Introduction may be brought to the reader's attention. One is Brentano's *Grundlegung und Aufbau der Ethik* (Bern: A. Francke, 1952), edited by Professor Franziska Mayer-Hillebrand of Innsbruck. This book was prepared from Brentano's notes for his lectures on Practical Philosophy, given at the University of Vienna from 1876 to 1894. It is now being translated into English by Elizabeth Schneewind. The other is Kraus's own *Die Werttheorien: Geschichte und Kritik* (Brünn: Richard M. Rohrer, 1937).

This is a most useful and informative discussion of the history of the theory of value up to the 1930's, seen from the point of view of the book that is here translated.

The present translation, which is completely new, was prepared by Elizabeth Schneewind and myself. To avoid confusion, we have retained the title that Cecil Hague used for his translation of the first edition. We wish to thank Miss Linda L. McAlister for a number of helpful suggestions and criticisms.

RODERICK M. CHISHOLM

*Brown University*

# *Author's Preface*

This lecture, which I now bring before a larger public, was given before the Vienna Law Society on January 23, 1889. At that time it was entitled "On the Natural Sanction for Law and Morality [*Von der natürlichen Sanktion für recht und sittlich*]". I have changed the title in order to make more clear just what the actual content of the lecture is. But otherwise I have made almost no changes at all. I have added numerous notes and appended one essay that had been previously published—namely, "Miklosich on Subjectless Propositions". Its bearing upon what may seem to be a very different subject matter will become evident in what follows.

The occasion of the lecture was an invitation from Baron von Hye, President of the Vienna Law Society. He asked me to present my own views on the subject that Ihering had discussed before the same society a few years earlier in a lecture entitled "On the Origin of the Sense of Justice [*Über die Entstehung des Rechtsgefühls*]". One should not infer, however, that the lecture is an incidental work prepared only for that particular occasion. I have tried to set forth the results of many years of reflection, which should be looked upon as a product of everything that I have published up to now.

What I have presented here is a part of a "Descriptive Psychology" which I hope to be able to publish in its entirety in the near future. This work will develop some of the views that were set forth in my *Psychology from an Empirical Standpoint* and will differ in fundamental respects from everything that has previously been said upon the subject. My readers will then be able to see,

I hope, that I have not been idle during the long period of my literary retirement.

Professional philosophers will see at once that there is much that is new in the present lecture. The rapidity with which I pass from one topic to another may conceal from the layman the sunken reefs that had to be circumnavigated. I have tried to be concise and therefore to keep in mind the counsel of Leibniz: pay little attention to refutation and much to demonstration. The notes I have added may give the reader some idea of the devious routes that others have taken and of what has kept them from finding a way out of the labyrinth. If these notes were to do justice to the subject, they would have to be multiplied a hundred-fold. Perhaps the reader will find what I have to say so obvious that he feels no debt to me at all. If this is so, it is all that I could ask. Indeed, I would look upon it as the crowning point of all my efforts.

I have attempted to determine the principles of our knowledge of ethics upon the basis of new analyses and in a way quite different from what has been done before. Other writers have also held that the feelings play an essential role in this knowledge. But unlike them I have broken radically and completely with the subjective view of ethics. I would make an exception only in the case of Herbart. But he became lost in the sphere of aesthetic feeling, and while remaining an irreconcilable enemy of contradiction in theoretical philosophy, he tolerated it in practical philosophy and assumed that our highest and universally valid ideas might there come into conflict with each other. Still his view is in certain respects very closely related to mine. And so, too, are other celebrated attempts to find a basis for ethics.

Some of the points made in the lecture are given a more precise statement in the notes; it would have been tedious to have developed them in the lecture itself. The notes also contain replies to objections, anticipated as well as actual. I hope that some will be interested in the historical contributions, particularly in the discussions of Descartes. I trace his theory of the evident back to its sources. And I point out two highly significant thoughts, one of which has been misunderstood and the other hardly noticed at all; neither has received the appreciation it deserves. I am referring, first, to his basic classification of psychological phenomena, and, secondly, to his view about the relation between joy and love and between hatred and sadness.

I have entered into a polemical debate with several contemporary investigators, all of whom are highly esteemed, no less by myself than by others. The sharpest remarks are directed towards those who have previously attacked my views and have thus compelled me to defend myself. I hope that they do not feel I am violating their own rights when I thus attempt, so far as I am able, to speak in behalf of the truth that we all serve. I have often spoken frankly, but I can assure my opponents, in all sincerity, of my wish that they will do the same.

FRANZ BRENTANO

# THE LECTURE

# The Origin of Our Knowledge of
# Right and Wrong

*1* The invitation to lecture which the Vienna Law Society extended to me was one that I could hardly refuse, for it gave expression in strong terms to a conviction which, unfortunately, seems to be on the point of disappearing. Proposals for a reform of legal studies have recently been heard (they are even said to have come from university circles) which can only spring from the belief that it is quite possible entirely to sever the roots of jurisprudence without the organism itself undergoing any injury at all. I am referring to the fact that the roots of jurisprudence are deeply implanted in practical philosophy and in the history of our country.

I must confess that, so far as history is concerned, I find these proposals completely incomprehensible. And so far as philosophy is concerned, I can find only this excuse: the men who occupy the chairs of our legal faculty have received a completely false impression of philosophy as a result of the confusions and incoherencies of the past few decades. No personal reproach is intended. But what if members of the medical faculty were to propose that their course of obligatory studies should be cut off entirely from zoology, physics, and chemistry?

In his *Vita a se ipso lineata*, Leibniz tells us this: "I found my previous studies of history and philosophy made it far easier for me to learn jurisprudence." In his *Specimen difficultatis in jure*, deploring the prejudices of the jurists of his time, he exclaims: "If only those who devote themselves to the study of law could overcome their contempt of philosophy and see that without

3

philosophy most of their questions would constitute a labyrinth without an exit!" What would he say now of these reform movements which can only set us back?

*2* The esteemed president of your society, who has preserved a vigorous and wide-ranging sense for the real scientific needs of his profession, made clear to me what it was that he would like to have me speak about. The question of the existence of a natural law, he said, was of special interest to the members of the society. And he himself was eager to learn my own opinion about the views that Ihering presented here some years ago.[1]

I consented gladly and have taken as my subject the natural sanction for law and morality. And I shall attempt to make clear the sole sense in which I believe that there is a natural law.

*3* The word "natural" may be used in two quite different ways:
(1) It may refer to what is "given by nature" or "innate", as distinguished from what has been acquired by experience or derived from the course of history.
(2) Or the word "natural" may refer to those rules which can be known to be correct and binding, in and for themselves, and in virtue of their own nature; rules that are "natural" in this sense contrast with the arbitrary dictates which those in power may happen to lay down.

Ihering rejects the concept of a natural law in each of these two senses.[2] I agree with him completely with respect to the first. And I disagree with him, just as completely, with respect to the second.

[1] Cf. Rudolf von Ihering, "*Über die Entstehung des Rechtsgefühles*", lecture delivered before the Vienna Law Society, March 12, 1884, published in *Allgem. Juristenzeitung*, Seventh Year, Number 11ff., Vienna, March 16–April 13, 1884. Compare Ihering's, *Der Zweck im Recht*, Vol. II (Leipzig, 1877–83).

[2] For the first point, see the *Allgem, Juristenzeitung*, Seventh Year, p. 122ff., and Ihering's *Zweck im Recht*, Vol. II, p. 109ff. For the second point, see the *Allgem. Juristenzeitung*, Seventh Year, p. 171, and *Zweck im Recht*, Vol. II, pp. 118–23. In the latter work, Ihering denies that there is any absolutely valid ethical rule (pp. 118, 122ff.) and he contests any "psychological" treatment of ethics which would represent ethics "as the twin sister of logic".

*4* I am thoroughly at one with Ihering when he says, following the example of John Locke, that there are no innate moral principles.

And like Ihering, I do not believe either in the baroque *jus naturae*, that law *quod natura ipsa omnia animalia docuit*, or in the *jus gentium*, that law which, as the Roman jurists taught, is supposed to be recognized as a natural law of reason by the universal agreement of all peoples.

One does not need to go very deeply into zoology and physiology to see that the animal world provides us with no criterion for setting up ethical standards. (In saying this, however, we do not need to go as far as Rokitansky who says that protoplasm, because of its aggressive character, is an unjust and evil principle!)

The doctrine that there is a common code of law for all nations may have been credible in the ancient world, but it is no longer so. Now that we know something about anthropology and the customs of more barbaric peoples, we realize that these laws are simply a product of the culture that is common to more advanced nations and that they are not a product of nature at all.

On this point, then, I am in complete agreement with Ihering. And I can agree in principle with his assertion that there have been times when there was no knowledge of right and wrong and no ethical feelings, or at any rate no ethical standard that was generally recognized.

Indeed, these conditions persisted even after the larger societies formed themselves into states. Ihering, in support of this view, points to the lack of moral thought among the gods and goddesses of Greek mythology and argues that one may draw inferences from the lives of these gods and goddesses to the lives of the people who formed the myths.[3] We may note, incidentally, that Aristotle had appealed to just this type of consideration in the *Politics*.[4] Ihering is certainly correct in maintaining that the earliest systems of law and of punishment were set up without the influence of anything like moral feelings or a sense of justice. No moral or legal precepts are "natural" in the sense of being implanted in us innately by nature itself. Ihering's views on this point have our complete approval.

[3] Ihering, *Allgem. Juristenzeitung*, Seventh Year, p. 147; compare his *Zweck im Recht*, Vol. II, p. 124ff.

[4] Aristotle, *Politics*, Book I, Ch. 2, 1252b 24.

*5* But now we must face the second question, which is far more important: Is there such a thing as a moral truth taught by nature itself and independent of ecclesiastical, political, and every other kind of social authority? Is there a moral law that is natural in the sense of being universally and incontestably valid—valid for men at all places and all times, indeed valid for any being that thinks and feels—and are we capable of knowing that there is such a law? This is the point at which I take issue with Ihering. He would answer the question negatively. My own answer is emphatically affirmative. I hope that the present inquiry into the natural sanction for law and morality will make clear which of us is right.

We cannot answer the present question merely by looking back to what we said about the former question—whatever Ihering himself may think to the contrary.[5] There are such things as innate prejudices. These are natural in the former sense, but they have no natural sanction; whether true or false, they possess no validity in themselves. On the other hand, there are many propositions which we come to know in a natural way and which are incontestably certain and universally valid for all thinking beings, and these propositions are anything but innate. An example is the Pythagorean theorem. (Had this theorem been innate, its happy discoverer would never have offered his hecatomb to the god.)

*6* It should be clear from what I have said how the term "sanction" is to be taken, when I speak of a natural sanction. We will do well, however, to consider the term in somewhat more detail, so that we may rule out a certain other inadequate conception.

"To sanction" is "to fix, establish, or make fast." Now a law may be fixed or established in two quite different senses.

(1) It may be fixed or established merely in the sense of becoming a law, as when it is ratified by the highest legislative authority.

(2) Or it may be fixed or established in the sense of being made more effective, as when it is combined with a system of rewards and punishments.

When the writers of antiquity spoke of sanctions, they took the term in the latter sense. Thus Cicero says of the leges Prociae:

---

[5] Cf. Ihering, *Allgem. Juristenzeitung*, Seventh Year, p. 146.

"Neque quicquam praeter sanctionem attulerunt novi."[6] And Ulpian says, similarly: "Interdum in sanctionibus adjicitur, ut, qui ibi aliquid commisit, capite puniatur."[7] In modern times, however, the term "sanction" is more likely to be taken in the first of these two senses. A law is said to be "sanctioned" when it has been laid down and made valid by the highest authorities. Quite obviously, the second sense of "sanction" presupposes the first. For if a law is not sanctioned in the first sense, it is not a law at all. The same thing will be true if there is a *natural* sanction for law and morality.*

7 And now we can easily see how philosophers have tended to overlook the essential character required of a natural sanction for morality.

8 Some suppose that we have discovered a natural sanction for a given type of conduct if we can show how it happens that the individual feels compelled to act that way. It may be, for example, that when we first render services to others we do so in the hope that we will receive similar services in return. We thus form the habit of performing such services and then we find that we are motivated to do so even when we have no thought of recompense.[8] Some would say that we have here the natural sanction for the duty to love one's neighbours.

But any such view is entirely wrong. A feeling of compulsion may well be a force that drives us to action, but it is not a sanction that confers validity. After all, the inclination to vice develops in

---

[6] Cicero, *Republica*, 2, 31.

[7] Ulpian, *Digest*, I, 8, 9.

[8] One of the most distinguished of the many adherents of this view is John Stuart Mill. See Chapter 3 of his *Utilitarianism*.

* [Editor's note: Since Brentano was speaking to a group of jurists and lawyers, he made use of the familiar legal term "sanction" to demonstrate his point. The comparison he had in mind was simply this: The laws of the state are valid, not because of the sanctions of punishment, but because they have been ratified by the highest legislative authority. Similarly, the rules of ethics are valid and binding, not because of any blind emotional impulse (section 8), or of motives stemming from hope and fear (section 9), or of any considerations pertaining to the will of a higher power or authority (section 10), but simply because of something akin to an intrinsic correctness.]

a similar way and this, too, becomes a compulsion which may exercise unlimited power. Or the miser may develop a passion which will lead him to undergo all kinds of sacrifices and to commit the most extreme of cruelties merely in order that he may amass his riches. But his passion hardly constitutes a sanction for his conduct.

*9* There are those who think that motives stemming from hope and fear constitute a natural sanction for certain types of conduct. Thus we may take an interest in the general good merely because we know that people in more powerful positions will look with favour upon certain types of action and with disfavour upon others.[9] If this sort of thing is a natural sanction, then so, too, are the lowest forms of flattery and cowardice [*die feigste Kriecherei, die servilste Speichelleckerei*]. But virtue proves itself most truly when neither threats nor promises can divert her from the path that she has set upon.

*10* Others speak of the way in which man as a social being may be brought up and educated by others. Again and again he hears the command "You ought!" It lies in the nature of things that certain types of action will continually be demanded of him. He thus tends to associate these types of action with the thought, "This is something that I ought to do." He then may come to regard the command as having its source in the society in which he lives, or in some ill-defined being more exalted than any particular person. It has been said that to look upon one's duty in this way is to be subject to the sanction of conscience.[10]

On such a view, the natural sanction for law and morality

[9] Here, too, John Stuart Mill may be cited, among others. He referred to the motives of hope and fear as *external* sanctions, and to the feelings of compulsion described earlier as *internal* sanctions. See Chapter 3 of *Utilitarianism*.

[10] See the discussion in James Mill's *Fragment on Mackintosh*, published in John Stuart Mill's edition (1869) of James Mill's *Analysis of the Phenomena of the Human Mind* (Chapter 23, pp. 309–21). See also Grote's ingenious essay, "On the Origin and Nature of Ethical Sentiment", published by A. Bain as the first essay in *Fragments on Ethical Subjects by the late George Grote F.R.S., being a Selection from his Posthumous Papers*, London 1876.

will be this conviction that moral commands have their source in some more powerful will. The conviction arises naturally enough, but it contains nothing that deserves to be called a sanction. A man who finds himself at the mercy of a tyrant or a gang of thieves knows that he is subject to commands that come from more powerful wills than his own. But whether or not he obeys, the commands do not impart to any act a sanction like that of conscience. If he does obey, he does so through fear and not because he believes the command to be one that is right.

An act does not have a natural sanction merely because it is thought to be commanded by someone. Of any command that is issued by an external will one may always ask: Is it justified or is it unjustified? And the question is not to be answered by looking for some still higher power which has issued a command enjoining obedience to the first command. If we are to obey the first command only if such obedience is demanded by a second command, then we should obey the second command only if such obedience is demanded by a third command, and so on *ad infinitum*.

A natural sanction for law and morality, then, cannot be found in the thought of a command of an external will, any more than it can be found in a feeling of compulsion or in the hope for reward or in the fear of retaliation.

*11* But there are commands or imperatives of an essentially different sort. For we may speak of the commands or imperatives of logic—commands and imperatives that pertain to judgement and inference. And here there is no question of any "will". These commands or imperatives do not have to do with the "will" of logic itself, since obviously it has none, or with the will of any logician to whom we may have sworn our allegiance. The laws of logic are rules of judging which are naturally valid. We are bound to conform to them, because such conformity ensures certainty in our judgements; if we fail to conform, our judgements become liable to error. In other words, thought processes that conform to these rules are naturally superior to those that do not. And so, too, in ethics. What we have in ethics are not the commands of an external will, but a natural superiority upon which the rules of morality are based. This is what Kant insisted upon, as did most of the great thinkers before him. But there are still many philosophers—unfortunately, even among those of the empirical school to which I myself belong—who do not correctly understand or appreciate this fact.

*12* What is this characteristic superiority which gives morality its natural sanction? There are those who have looked upon it as being, so to speak, external, for they have taken it to be the superiority of a beautiful appearance. The Greeks said that noble and virtuous conduct is τὸ καλόν, or beautiful, and they described the complete man of honour as being καλοκάγαθός. These ancient thinkers, however, did not mean to set up an *aesthetic* criterion of what is moral and what is not. Unfortunately this cannot be said of certain modern thinkers. Thus in England, David Hume spoke of a moral sense of beauty which enables us to decide what is moral and what is not.[11] And in Germany Herbart has more recently argued that ethics is a branch of aesthetics.[12]

I certainly do not deny that the appearance of virtue is more agreeable than that of moral perversity. But the essential superiority of what is moral does not *consist* in this fact. A will that is moral is *intrinsically* superior or preferable to one that is immoral—in just the way in which evident judgements and correct inferences are intrinsically superior to prejudice and to fallacious reasoning. It cannot be denied that there is something ugly and small about prejudice and fallacious reasoning. It is not especially agreeable to contemplate people who are prone to these things. But this hardly means that the laws of logic are rules of aesthetics, or that logic is itself a branch of aesthetics.[13] The essential superiority that concerns us does not consist in any

[11] David Hume, *An Inquiry concerning the Principles of Morals*, London 1751.

[12] J. F. Herbart, *Lehrbuch zur Einleitung in die Philosophie* in *Sämtliche Werke*, ed. Hartenstein, Leipzig 1850-2, Vol. I, Sect. 81ff., p. 127ff.

[13] The accusation that I have misrepresented Herbart's views is best answered by reference to the comparison I have made between ethics and logic. The logical criterion, I have said, involves the inner evidence of thought processes that conform to rules; it does not consist of the judgements of taste that we make when we contemplate such processes and compare them with those that do not conform to rules. If the logical criterion were to consist of such judgements, then it could be described as external. And it is just in this sense that Herbart's

aesthetic appearance; it is, rather, a certain intrinsic correctness which, however, may also *have* a certain superiority in appearance. Similarly, it is a certain intrinsic correctness which makes one act of will superior to another and which therefore makes the difference between what is moral and what is not.

*Belief* in this intrinsic superiority or preferability is an ethical motive. *Knowledge* of it is the *correct* ethical motive and the sanction which gives permanence and validity to the moral law.

*13* But how do we attain such knowledge?

Here we find a difficulty which philosophers have sought in vain to resolve. Even Kant felt that no one prior to him had found the proper way of untying the knot. He thought that he himself had found it in the Categorical Imperative. Actually, however, the Categorical Imperative is like the sword drawn by Alexander to cut the Gordian knot. It is a palpable fiction and is not what is needed to set the matter right.[14]

*14* To understand the true source of our ethical knowledge, we must consider the results of recent investigations in the area of descriptive psychology. The limited time that I have requires me to be very brief in setting forth my own views. I am afraid, therefore, that my statement will not be as complete as it ought to be. But it is just here that I would like to ask for your special attention in order that we may not lose sight of what is essential to a proper understanding of our problem.

*15* The will is that which is said to be moral or immoral. In many cases what we will is only a means to some further end. In such cases, we also will the end and, in a certain sense, we will it more than we do the means. The end itself may, in turn, be a means to some further end. In any far-reaching plan, there will be a whole series of ends, each end subordinate to the one to which it is itself

---

[14] [This note, "On Kant's Categorical Imperative", may be found on page 49f.]

---

criterion in ethics may be said to be external—even though Herbartians may insist that the judgements of taste we form spontaneously upon contemplation of certain acts of will reveal the intrinsic superiority of those acts.

a means. But there must always be some end which is desired above all the others and for itself alone. If there were no such strict and ultimate end, there would be no incentive in pursuing the rest of the plan. We would be in the absurd position of aiming without having anything to aim at.

*16* We may employ various means in order to bring about a particular end. Some of them will be correct and others not. They will be correct when they are really suitable for bringing about the end.

We may also have a variety of ultimate ends. A common mistake in the eighteenth century, much less prevalent today, was to believe that everyone seeks the same end—namely, the greatest possible pleasure for himself.[15] We have only to think of those martyrs who submitted to the most excruciating of tortures for the sake of their convictions, very often without having any hope of recompense in a life hereafter. No one who is familiar with the facts supposes that these people were really trying to maximize their own pleasure (no one, at least, who has any sense of the intensity of pleasure and of pain).

This, therefore, is certain: there is a variety of ultimate ends. We must choose among them. And since the ultimate end that we adopt is the determining principle for everything else, the choice of ultimate ends is the most important choice of all. What ought I to strive after? Which end is correct and which one incorrect? As Aristotle said, this is the fundamental question of ethics.[16]

*17* What end is the correct one? What end ought we to choose?

Once the ultimate end has been determined and we are choosing merely among possible means, then the proper reply is: Choose those means that will actually bring about the end. But

---

[15] Compare John Stuart Mill, *System of Deductive and Inductive Logic*, Book IV, Chapter 4, Section 6 (toward the end) and Book VI, Chapter 2, Section 4, and elsewhere: for example, in *Utilitarianism*, *Essays on Religion*, and *Auguste Comte and Positivism*, Part II.

[16] Comparison with the first chapter of the *Nicomachaean Ethics* shows that Ihering's "basic idea"—viz., that "every legal maxim has its origin in some goal" (*Der Zweck im Recht*, Vol. I, p. vi)—is as old as ethics itself.

where the choice is among ends themselves, then one might say: Choose an end that can reasonably be thought of as being attainable. But this answer is hardly enough. For many things that can be attained are to be avoided rather than sought after. Choose *the best* among the ends that are attainable: this is the only adequate answer.[17]

But the answer is obscure. What do we mean by "the best"? What do we call "good"? And how do we find out that a given thing is good or that one thing is better than another?

*18* To answer these questions, we must inquire into the origin of our concept of the good. This concept, like all our others, has its origin in certain intuitive presentations.[18]

Some of our intuitive presentations have *physical* content. These

---

[17] When the prospect of success is doubtful, we may have to choose between two courses: the one offering a greater good but less probability of success and the other offering a lesser good but a greater probability of success. In such cases, we must take account of the respective probabilities. If A is three times better than B, but B has ten times more chances of being realized than does A, then the man of practical wisdom will prefer to strive after B. For if such a course were always pursued under such circumstances, and if there were a sufficient number of cases, then, given the law of large numbers, the greater good would be realized on the whole. And therefore such a procedure would conform to the principle that I have expressed: Choose the best among the ends that are attainable. The point of this observation will become clearer in what follows. [Editor's note: Compare the short essay on Benjamin Franklin in the Appendix.]

[18] This truth was known to Aristotle (see, for example, *De Anima*, Book III, Chapter 8). It was also recognized by medieval thinkers, but they expressed it somewhat ineptly, in the dictum: *nihil est in intellectu, quod non prius fuerit in sensu.* The concepts of *willing* and *inferring* are not drawn from *sense* perception. If we were to call them sense concepts, we would have to take the term "sense" so generally that we could no longer make any distinction between what is sensible and what is not. But these concepts do have their origin in certain concrete intuitions that have a psychological content. This is how we acquire the concept of *end* or *purpose*. The concept of *cause* has a similar origin (we note, for example, a causal relation between our belief in a set of premises and our belief in the conclusion). So do the concepts of *impossibility* and *necessity*. (We acquire these by making what are called "apodictic"

13

present us with sense qualities that are spatially determined in a characteristic way. They constitute the source of our concepts of colour, sound, space, and the like. But the concept of the good does not have its origin here. The concept of the good has been associated quite properly with the concept of the true. It is easy to see that both concepts have their origin in certain intuitive presentations having psychological content.*

19 The common feature of everything psychological, often referred to, unfortunately, by the misleading term "consciousness", consists in a relation that we bear to an object. The relation has been called *intentional*; it is a relation to something which may not be actual but which is presented as an object.[19] There is no hearing unless something is heard, no believing unless something is believed; there is no hoping unless something is hoped for, no striving unless something is striven for; one cannot be pleased unless there is something that one is pleased about; and so on, for all the other psychological phenomena.†

20 Those intuitive presentations that have *physical* content may be distinguished in a variety of ways. By reference to the basic

[19] A suggestion of this view may be found in Aristotle; see especially *Metaphysics*, Book V, Chapter 15, 1021a 29. The expression "intentional", like many other terms for our more important concepts, comes from the scholastics.

* [Editor's note: Brentano was later to drop this use of "content (*Inhalt*)" in favour of "objeots (*Objekte*)".]

† [Editor's note: But one should not take Brentano to be saying that psychological attitudes and their objects are correlative entities both of which must exist; for the objects of psychological attitudes need not exist. See Brentano's *Psychology from an Empirical Standpoint*, Vol. II, Appendix I.]

judgements—those judgements which affirm or deny, not merely assertorically, but also apodictically). And similarly for many other concepts which some modern philosophers, failing to discover their true source, have tried to interpret as being *a priori* categories. (I am aware that Sigwart and others influenced by him have called into question the distinction between assertoric and apodictic, but this is not the place to discuss such psychological errors. See the discussion of Sigwart, in Note 27, "On the Evident", on page 76ff.)

14

distinctions among sense qualities (what Helmholtz refers to as distinctions of modality), we may determine the number of different senses. [And those intuitive presentations that have *psychological* content may also be distinguished in a variety of ways. By reference to the basic distinctions among intentional relations, we may determine the number of basic psychological categories.[20]

We may thus distinguish three fundamental classes of psychological phenomena. It was Descartes who first made this distinction; we find a complete and accurate statement in the *Meditations*.[21] But what he said was not sufficiently attended to and it was soon forgotten. In more recent times, Descartes' method of classification was independently rediscovered, and we may now look upon it as something that has been established.[22]

The first fundamental class, Descartes' *ideae*, is that of ideas in the broadest sense of this term, or, as we may also call them, presentations [*Vorstellungen*]. This includes the concrete intuitive presentations that are given to us through the senses along with those concepts that are not properly called sensible.

[The second fundamental class, Descartes' *judicia*, is that of judgement. Before Descartes' time, judgements and presentations were grouped together as constituting a *single* fundamental class. The same error has been made in more recent times; people have supposed that judging is essentially a matter of combining or relating presentations. But this is a gross misconception of the nature of judgement. On the one hand, we may combine and relate presentations at will—as we do when we think of a green tree, or a golden mountain, or a father of a hundred children, or a

[20] For a more adequate discussion, see my *Psychology from an Empirical Standpoint*, Book II, Chapter 6 (in Vol. II); compare also Book II, Chapter 1, Section 5 (Vol. I). Except for certain points of detail, I believe that what I say there about the classification of psychological phenomena is substantially correct. [Editor's note: These points of detail are discussed in the Supplementary Essays to be found in Volume Two of Brentano's *Psychology*.]

[21] [This note, "On Descartes' Classification of Psychological Phenomena", may be found on page 5 off.]

[22] [This note, "In Defense of a Theory of Judgement", may be found on page 54ff.]

friend of science—but if we have *only* combined and related, we have made no *judgement*. (To be sure, every judgement is based upon some presentation or other and so, too, is every desire.) And on the other hand, we may make a judgement without thereby combining ideas or relating them as subject and predicate. Thus consider the judgement "There is a God", as distinguished, say, from "God is just".

What is distinctive about judgement? It is this: In addition to there being an idea or presentation of a certain object, there is a second intentional relation which is directed upon that object. The relation is one of either affirmation or denial—either acceptance or rejection. If a man says "God", he gives expression to the idea of God. But if he says "There is a God", then he gives expression to his belief in God.

I must not linger here. But I can assure you that if there is any point that is now beyond doubt, it is this. Miklosich has given us a philological confirmation of the results of this psychological analysis.[23]

The third fundamental class consists of the emotions in the widest sense of this term. These include, not only the simplest forms of inclination and disinclination which may arise from the mere *thought* of an object, but also the joy or sorrow that is grounded in the *beliefs* that we have, as well as the highly complicated phenomena that are involved in ends and means. Aristotle had included these under his term ὄρεξις. Descartes said that this class includes the *voluntates sive affectus*. Where the second class involves an intentional relation of either affirmation or denial (either acceptance or rejection), the third class involves an intentional relation of love or hate, or (as we may also put it) inclination or disinclination, being pleased or being displeased. This relation is in the simplest forms of inclination and disinclination, in victorious joy and despairing sorrow, in hope and fear, and in every act of will. The French ask "Plaît-il?" The Germans say, in their announcements of death, "Es hat Gott gefallen." And one writes "Placet" as the verbal confirmation of a decisive decree of the will.[24]

[23] [This note, "On Existential and Negative Judgements", may be found on page 59ff.]

[24] In his valuable little book *The Passions of the Soul* [in the *Philosophical Works of Descartes*, trans. E. S. Haldane and G. R. T. Ross,

16

*21* Comparison of these three classes of phenomena reveals that the last two exhibit a certain analogy that is not shared by the first. The last two but not the first involve an opposition of intentional relation. In the case of judgement there is the opposition between affirmation or acceptance, on the one hand, and denial or rejection, on the other. In the case of the emotions there is the opposition between love and hate or, as we may also put it, the opposition between inclination and disinclination, between being pleased and being displeased. But in the case of mere presentation—in the mere having of an idea—there is no such opposition. Of course, I may think of things which are opposites—for example, black and white—but there are not opposite ways of thinking of these things. There are two opposing ways of *judging* about a black thing and two opposing ways of feeling about it, but there are not two opposing ways of merely thinking about it.

*22* This fact has an important consequence. Psychological acts that belong to the first class cannot be said to be either correct or incorrect. But in the case of the acts that belong to the second class, one of the two opposing modes of relation—affirmation and denial—is correct and the other is incorrect, as logic has taught since ancient times. Naturally, the same thing is true of the third class. Of the two opposing types of feeling—loving and hating, inclination and disinclination, being pleased and being

---

Vol. I] Descartes comes very close to saying that love is always a matter of "being pleased" and hatred a matter of "being displeased". Thus he writes in Part Two, Article 139: ". . . when the things which they [love and hate] persuade us to love are truly good, and those which [they] persuade us to hate are truly evil, love is incomparably better than hate: it can never be too great, and it never fails to produce joy." And this accords with what he says a little later (Article 140): "Hate, on the contrary, can never be so small that it is not injurious, and it is never without sorrow."

Ordinarily one does not use the expressions "joy" and "sorrow", or "pleasure" and "displeasure", unless the feeling has reached a certain degree of intensity. We may make use of this pre-scientific distinction, despite the fact that it offers us no sharp boundary-line, provided we place no such limitation upon the expressions "being pleased [*gefallen*]" and "being displeased [*missfallen*]".

17

displeased—in every instance one of them is correct and the other incorrect.*

**23** And now we have found what we have been looking for. We have arrived at the source of our concepts of the good and the bad, along with that of our concepts of the true and the false. We call a thing *true* when the affirmation relating to it is correct.[25] We call a thing *good* when the love relating to it is correct. In the broadest sense of the term, the good is that which is worthy of love, that which can be loved with a love that is correct.

**24** Among the things that please us, we may distinguish between those that are pleasing in themselves and those that are pleasing in virtue of something else. In the latter case, the thing is pleasing in virtue of what it brings about or preserves or makes probable. Hence we must distinguish between primary and secondary goods—between what is good in itself and what is good in virtue of something else. The useful is a clear example of the latter type of good.

Taking the term "good" in its narrow sense, we may equate the good with the good in itself. It is only the good in itself that can stand side by side with the true. For whatever is true is true in itself, even though it may be known in virtue of something else. Henceforth, when I speak of the good I shall be referring to the good in itself (unless I explicitly say otherwise).

So much, then, for the concept of the good.[26]

**25** And now we arrive at an even more important question: How are we to *know* that a thing is good? Should we say that whatever is loved or is capable of being loved is something that

[25] [This note, "On the Concepts of Truth and Existence", may be found on page 73 ff.]

[26] [This note, "On the Unity of the Concept of the Good", may be found on page 75 ff.]

* [Editor's note: Brentano was later to modify this view. According to his later view, the emotions differ from judgement in that "not correct", in the sphere of the emotions, does not imply "incorrect", and "not incorrect" does not imply "correct". See his posthumous *Die Lehre vom richtigen Urteil* (Bern: Francke Verlag, 1956), ed. F. Mayer-Hillebrand, p. 175 ff. R.M.C.]

18

is worthy of love and therefore good? Obviously this would not be right, and it is almost impossible to comprehend how it could be that some have fallen in to such an error. One person loves what another hates. And, in accordance with a well-known psychological law already touched upon in this lecture, it often happens as a result of habit that what is at first desired merely as a means to something else comes to be desired for itself alone. Thus the miser is reduced to heaping up riches irrationally and even to sacrificing himself in order to acquire them. And so we may say that the fact that a thing is loved is no indication that it is worthy of being loved—just as we may say that the fact that something is affirmed or accepted is no indication that it is true.

Indeed, of these two statements, the former is the more obvious. It is hardly possible for a man to accept or affirm something and at the same time hold it to be false. But it may frequently happen that one loves something that one admits to be unworthy of such love:

> "Video meliora proboque,
> Deteriora sequor."

How then, are we to know that a thing is good?

26 The matter may now seem very puzzling, but there is a simple solution.

To prepare the answer, let us consider once again the analogy that holds between the good and the true.

The fact that we affirm something does not mean that it is true, for we often judge quite blindly. Many of the prejudices that we acquired in our infancy may take on the appearance of indubitable principles. And all men have by nature an impulse to trust certain other judgements that are equally blind—for example, those judgements that are based upon so-called external perception and those that are based upon memories of the recent past. What is affirmed in this way may often be true, but it is just as likely to be false. For these judgements involve nothing that manifests correctness.

But they may be contrasted with certain other judgements which are "insightful" or "evident". The law of contradiction is one example. Other examples are provided by so-called inner perception, which tells me that I am now having such-and-such sound or colour sensations, or that I am now thinking or willing this or that.

What, then, is the essential distinction between these lower and higher forms of judgement? Is it a distinction with respect to degree of conviction or is it something else? It does not pertain to degree of conviction. Many of those blind, instinctive assumptions that arise out of habit are completely uninfected by doubt. Some of them are so firmly rooted that we cannot get rid of them even after we have seen that they have no logical justification. But they are formed under the influence of obscure impulses; they do not have the clarity that is characteristic of the higher form of judgement. If one were to ask, "Why do you really believe that?", it would be impossible to find any rational grounds. Now if one were to raise the same question in connection with a judgement that is immediately evident, here, too, it would be impossible to refer to any grounds. But in this case the clarity of the judgement is such as to enable us to see that the question has no point; indeed, the question would be completely ridiculous. Everyone experiences the difference between these two classes of judgement. As in the case of every other concept, the ultimate explication consists only in a reference to this experience.

27 In its essentials, all this is universally recognized.[27] Only a few have contested it, and then with great inconsistency. Less notice has been taken of the analogous distinction between the higher and lower types of activity in the emotional sphere, in the sphere of inclination and disinclination.

The feelings of inclination and disinclination often resemble blind judgement in being only instinctive or habitual. This is so in the case of the pleasure the miser takes in hoarding money as well as in those powerful feelings of pleasure and displeasure that men and animals alike connect with the appearance of certain sensuous qualities.* Moreover, different species and even different

[27] [This note, "On the Evident", may be found on pages 76ff.]

* [Editor's note: A detailed statement of Brentano's view about the relations between the emotions and their sensuous side-effects (*Redundanzen*), may be found in his *Untersuchungen zur Sinnespsychologie* (Leipzig: Duncker & Humblot, 1907), pp. 119–25. Compare also

individuals are often affected in contrary ways; this is obvious, of course, in connection with matters of taste.

Many philosophers, and among them very significant thinkers, have taken into account only that mode of pleasure that is peculiar to the lower types of activity within the sphere of the emotions. They have entirely overlooked the fact that there is a higher mode of being pleased or displeased. Thus in almost every word David Hume betrays the fact that he has no idea at all of this higher class.[28] We can see how widespread this oversight has been when we realize that none of the words of ordinary language are intended to be adequate to the distinction.[29] But the fact is undeniable. We may elucidate it by a few examples.

As I have said, it is natural for us to take pleasure in certain tastes and to feel an antipathy toward others. In both cases, our

---

[28] [This note, "Ethical Subjectivism", may be found on pages 84ff.]

[29] In saying that our ordinary language does not contain any expressions that are suitable to those emotional activities which are experienced as being correct, I do not mean to deny that there are certain expressions which would lend themselves quite well to the purpose and which, indeed, almost seem to have been made for it. Thus there are the expressions "*gut gefallen*" ("to please well") and "*schlecht gefallen*" ("to please ill"), as distinct from the simpler "*gefallen*" ("to please") and "*misfallen*" ("to displease"). We might wish to restrict the use of the former pair of expressions and make technical terms of them, but we would find almost no trace of such a restriction in ordinary language. One would not want to say that the good pleases him ill (*das Gute gefällt ihm schlecht*) or that the bad pleases him well (*das Schlechte gefällt ihm gut*). But we do say that a thing may "taste good" to one man and "taste bad" to another. And we do not hesitate to say "feels good" in the case of the lowest instinctive pleasures. The term "perception" ("*Wahrnehmung*") has degenerated in very much the same way. Though it is applicable in the strict sense only to cases of knowledge, it has come to be applied also, in connection with so-called "external perception", to cases of blind and essentially erroneous belief. It would not be a useful technical term unless we could institute a basic reform in our ordinary terminology and drastically limit its sphere of applicability.

---

Brentano's *Vom sinnlichen und noetischen Bewusstsein* (Leipzig: Felix Meiner, 1928), pp. 16–17, 80–1, 138–9; this latter work is sometimes referred to as "*Psychologie*, Vol. III."]

feelings are purely instinctive. But it is also natural for us to take pleasure in the clarity of insight and to feel displeased by error or ignorance. "All men", Aristotle says in the beautiful introductory words to the *Metaphysics*, "naturally desire knowledge".[30] This desire is an example which will serve our purpose. It is a pleasure of the highest form; it it thus the analogue of something being evident in the sphere of judgement. It is a pleasure that is common to all the members of our species. Imagine now another species quite different from ourselves; not only do its members have preferences with respect to sense qualities which are quite different from ours; unlike us, they also despise insight and love error for its own sake. So far as the feelings about sense qualities are concerned, we might say that these things are a matter of taste, and *"De gustibus non est disputandum"*. But this is not what we would say of the love of error and the hatred of insight. We would say that such love and hatred are basically perverse and that the members of the species in question hate what is indubitably and intrinsically good and love what is undubitably and intrinsically bad. Why do we answer differently in the two cases when the feeling of compulsion is equally strong? The answer is simple. In the former case the feeling of compulsion is merely instinctive. But in the latter case the natural feeling of pleasure is a higher love that is experienced as being correct. When we ourselves experience such a love we notice not only that its object is loved and capable of being loved, and that its privation or contrary hated and capable of being hated, but also that the one is worthy of love and the other worthy of hate, and therefore that the one is good and the other bad.

Let us consider another example. Just as we prefer insight to error, so, too, generally speaking, we prefer joy to sadness—unless it be joy in what is bad. Were there beings who preferred things the other way around, we would take their attitudes to be perverse, and rightly so. For here, too, our love and hatred are experienced as being correct.

A third example may be found in those very feelings that are correct and are experienced as being correct. The correctness and higher character of these feelings—like the correctness and

[30] *Metaphysics*, Book I, Chapter I, 930a 22.

22

evidence of certain judgements—is itself to be counted as something that is good. And love of the bad is something that is itself bad.[31]

In order not to leave unmentioned the corresponding experiences in the sphere of ideas or presentations, we should note that every act of thought—that is to say, every instance of having an idea or presentation—is something that is good in itself. And the good within us is increased with every extension of our thought, regardless of what good or harm may result therefrom.[32]

[31] To avoid misunderstanding, I add the following to what has only been sketched in the text. For an emotive act to be purely good in itself it must be such that (1) it is correct and (2) it is an instance of being pleased and not one of being displeased. If either condition is lacking, then the act is in some respect intrinsically bad in itself. Pleasure in the misfortunes of others (*Schadenfreude*) is bad because it fails to meet the first condition; the pain that we take in the sight of injustice is bad because it fails to meet the second. If both conditions are lacking, then the emotive act is still worse. This accords with the principle of summation which is taken up later in the lecture. The principle tells us that if a feeling is good, then if the feeling is increased, the goodness of the act is also increased. Similarly, if an act is purely bad, or even if it is bad only in some respects, then the badness of the act increases with the intensity of the feeling. If the act is a mixed one, then good and bad increase or diminish in direct proportion to one another. The plus which belongs to one side or the other becomes greater with an increase in the intensity of the act, and smaller with a decrease in the intensity of the act. Hence under certain circumstances a predominance of good in the act can be described as a very great good, even if the act is not purely good. And conversely, what is predominantly bad may be described as something that is itself very bad even if there is an admixture of the good. Compare note 37 below [pages 90ff.].

[32] It can happen that a given thing may both please and displease us, at one and the same time. Thus what may displease us in itself may yet please us as a means to something else, and conversely. And it may happen that, though we are instinctively repelled by a certain thing, we love it at the same time with a higher type of love. Thus we may have an instinctive repugnance toward a sensation which, all the same, is a welcome enrichment to the world of our ideas—every act of thought being something which as such is good in itself. Aristotle remarked: "It sometimes occurs that desires enter into conflict with each other. This happens when reason (λόγος) and the lower desires (ἐπιθυμία) are opposed." (*De Anima*, Book III, Chapter 10.

23

Our knowledge of what is truly and indubitably good arises from the type of experience we have been discussing, where a love is experienced as being correct—in all those cases where we are capable of such knowledge.[33]

We should note, however, that there is no guarantee that every good thing will arouse in us an emotion that is experienced as being correct. When this does not occur, our criterion fails, in which case the good is absent so far as our knowledge and practical purposes are concerned.[34]

[33] Love and hate may be directed upon entire classes as well as upon single individuals, as Aristotle had noted. We are angry, he said, only with the particular thief who has robbed us, or with the particular sycophant who has deceived us in our innocence, but we hate thieves and sycophants in general (*Rhetoric*, Book II, Chapter 4, 1382a). Acts of love and hate which are thus based upon some general concept are also frequently experienced as being correct. And then, along with the experience of the given act of love or hate, the goodness or badness of the entire class becomes obvious at a single stroke, so to speak, and without any induction from particular cases. This is the way, for example, that we attain to the general knowledge that insight as such is good. Since we have here the apprehension of a general truth without the induction from particular cases that is required to establish other empirical propositions, some philosophers have been tempted to look upon the universal judgement as a synthetic *a priori* form of immediate knowledge. The temptation is easy to understand. But it overlooks the fact that the apprehension of such a general truth is preceded by an emotion that is experienced as being correct. Herbart has a remarkable doctrine to the effect that one is suddenly elevated to a knowledge of general ethical principles; I suspect that he noticed something of this unique process but without becoming entirely clear about it. [Editor's note: See Appendix I, "Ethical Principles as A Priori"; compare also Brentano's *Psychologie vom empirischen Standpunkt*, Vol. II, Appendix VII.]

[34] It is easy to see how important this fact could be for a theodicy. One might fear, however, that it threatens to undermine ethics, if not to demolish it altogether. But such a fear is unfounded: see note 44 below.

433b 5–12). And again: "Sometimes the lower desires gain a victory over the higher, sometimes the higher over the lower. Just as one celestial sphere draws along another [according to ancient astronomy], so one desire carries the other off with it when the individual loses firm control over himself." (*De Anima*, Book III, Chapter 11, 434a 12–14.)

24

28 But there are many things, and not just a single thing, that we recognize in this manner to be good. Hence we are left with the questions: Among the things that are good, and more particularly among those goods that are attainable, which ones are better than others? And which of them is the highest practical good? We must be able to answer this latter question if we are to learn what the end is that we ought to strive after.

29 And so we should ask first: When is one thing *better* than another and known by us to be better? And what is meant by "the better"?

Although the answer is at hand, there is one possible error that we must exclude. Since the good is that which is worthy of being loved for its own sake, one might take the better to be that which is worthy of a *greater* love for its own sake. But is this really so? What is supposed to be meant by "a greater love"? Is it a spatial magnitude? This could hardly be. Inclination and disinclination —being pleased and displeased—are not measured in feet and inches. Perhaps someone will say that the intensity of the feeling of pleasure is what he has in mind when he speaks of "a greater love". In this case the better would be what pleases more intensely. But this is ridiculous. It would imply that for each instance of rejoicing only a certain amount of joy is appropriate. But surely it can never be reprehensible to feel the greatest joy possible in what is good, to enjoy it, as we say, with all one's heart. Descartes observed that the act of love when it is directed upon what is really good can never be too intense.[35] And he was obviously right. Otherwise think of the care we should have to exercise in view of the limitations of our mental strength! Every time we might wish to rejoice over something good, we would have to take an anxious survey over all the other things we know to be good in order to make sure that our joy does not exceed the proper proportions. And what if one believes in a God, understanding thereby the infinite good and ideal of all ideals? The degree of our love for God can only be of a certain finite intensity even if we love him with all our soul and all our strength. Hence we would be compelled to love any *other* good

[35] See the passage quoted in note [page 17].

25

with an infinitely small degree of intensity, and since this is not possible, we would be obliged not to love it at all.

And this is clearly absurd.

*30* Nonetheless it is true that the better is that which it is correct to love more; it is that in which one correctly takes more pleasure. But the "more" has nothing to do with comparative intensity. It refers to a peculiar type of phenomenon to be found within the sphere of the emotions—namely, to the phenomenon of *preferring*. Acts of preference—emotive acts that relate and compare—are familiar to us all. There is nothing similar in the sphere of ideas or presentations. The sphere of judgement does include acts of relating and comparing; these are exemplified, not in simple, subjectless judgements, but in predicative judgements. But the analogy to preference is only slight. We come somewhat closer to preference when we consider what is involved in making a decision with respect to the dialectically proposed question: "Is this true or is it false?" In this case, there is certainly a kind of preference. But it is always a matter of preferring something true to something false; it is never a matter of preferring something "more true" to something "less true". Everything that is true is equally true; but not everything that is good is equally good. When we call one good "better" than another, we mean that the one good is preferable to the other. In other words, it is *correct to prefer* the one good, for its own sake, to the other. Using language somewhat more broadly, we also permit ourselves to say that what is good is "better" than what is bad, or "better" than what is purely indifferent. We may even say that one bad thing is "better" than another—in which case, we are permitting ourselves to call the one thing "better" without implying thereby that it is good.

Very briefly, then, this is the way we explicate the concept of the better.

*31* And now to the question: How do we come to know that one thing is better than another?

Given that we have an elementary knowledge of what is good and of what is bad, analogy would suggest that we derive our insights about better from acts of *preferring* that are experienced as being correct. Preference is like the simple act of love or in-

26

clination in being sometimes of a lower type and thus merely compulsive, and sometimes of a higher type; in the latter case, preference, like the evident judgement, is distinguished as being correct. Some would say, perhaps justifiably, that when preference is thus seen to be correct, certain analytic judgements about preference are the source of the knowledge that is involved. If this is so, then the acts of preference themselves would not be the empirical source of our knowledge about preferability. Rather, we would appeal to what we already know about the nature of preferability in order to be able to see that certain acts of preference are correct.[36]

The most prominent cases of this kind are (1) those in which we prefer something that is good and known to be good to something that is bad and known to be bad. And then there are (2) those cases in which we prefer the existence of something that is known to be good to its non-existence, and in which we

[36] The following seems to me to be evident even simply on the basis of analysis of the concept of preferring. (1) To the extent that a thing is good, it should be weighed in the balance as a positive factor. (2) To the extent that a thing is bad, it should be weighed in the balance as a negative factor. And therefore (3) when the outcome is a function just of the greater preponderance, as in those cases discussed in the lecture, we determine which thing is preferable, partly by immediate insight into what is good and what is bad and partly by doing a sum in which the good and the bad are given opposite signs. In such cases, therefore, we can find out which things are better without the need of any act of preference that is experienced as being correct; we need only to experience the relevant acts of love and hate, inclination and disinclination, as being correct. And this is why I have said above that we need not derive our knowledge of preferability from the fact that our acts of preference are experienced as being correct. We may make use of what we know about the nature of preferability and can thereby see that certain acts of preference are correct. But in saying this, I do not mean to deny that acts of preference, like the simpler acts of love and hate, may be experienced by us as being correct. [Editor's note: Brentano was later to modify the views set forth in this note. He saw that, in order to find out that one thing is preferable to another, it is necessary not only to experience certain acts of love and hate and to appeal to analytic judgements about the nature of preference; one must also experience certain acts of preference. See Anton Marty's sketch of Brentano's life and work in Marty's *Gesammelte Schriften*, Volume I, Section I (Halle: Max Niemeyer, 1916), pp. 97–103.]

prefer the non-existence of something that is known to be bad to its existence.

This second category includes a number of different types of case. There is the case in which we prefer, in itself, something that is purely good to that same good in combination with something that is bad. There is the case in which we prefer, in itself, a combination of what is good and what is bad to that same bad without the admixture of anything that is good. And there are the cases where, given a whole that is good, we prefer the whole to a part, and where, given a whole that is bad, we prefer a part to the whole. Aristotle called attention to the fact that the total sum of what is good is always better than the particular parts that make it up. Summation is also involved when we consider lengths of time. A feeling of joy that lasts for an hour is better than a similar feeling of joy that is extinguished after only a moment. Epicurus denies this when he tries to console us for being mortal, but the consequences of his view are manifestly absurd. If he were right, an hour's torture would be no worse than that of a moment. And it would follow from these two things together that a life full of joy with but a single moment of pain would be in no way preferable to a brief life full of pain with but a single moment of joy. But no reasonable person could accept this, and Epicurus himself also explicitly asserts the contrary.

(3) The third category is closely related to the second. We may prefer one good to another if the second good, though not itself a part of the first, is similar in every respect to some part of the first. If by adding one good to another we obtain a sum which is better than its parts, then so, too, when we add to the first good a good that is similar in every respect to the second good. And analogously for what is bad. If on one occasion we see a beautiful painting in its entirety and if on another we see it in a similar way but only in part, then the first experience is intrinsically better than the second. Or compare two different acts of thought: on one occasion we merely think of a certain thing that is good and on another occasion we think about it, just as fully, and we also love it as well. The sum of psychical acts—the thinking and the loving together—is better than the thinking alone.

Cases exhibiting differences in degree also belong to this third class, and they are especially worthy of mention. If one good, say an experience of joy, is in every respect like another except for being more intense than the other, then the preference that is given to the one that is more intense is experienced as being correct; the more intense one is the better. And conversely, the more intense of two evils, the more intensive pain, for example, is the worse. The degree of intensity corresponds to the distance from the zero point, and the distance of the greater degree of intensity from the zero point may be thought of as a sum comprising the distance of the weaker degree of intensity from the zero point taken together with the difference between the stronger and weaker degrees of intensity. And so (even though the point has been disputed) we are really concerned with a kind of summation here.

*32* Some may find the three cases I have set forth so obvious and trivial that they wonder why I have spent any time with them. I agree that they are obvious, for we are dealing here with the foundations of our subject. It would be worse if I had to say that they were trivial, since they are just about the only cases I can mention. There are simply no criteria for most of the other cases of correct preference.[37]

Let us consider an example. Every insight, we have said, is something that is good in itself. Every act of high-minded love is also something that is good in itself. There is no doubt whatever about either of these things. But which of the two is intrinsically better—the insight or the act of love? There are, of course, people who are quite ready to issue a verdict on this point. Some have even said that any given instance of high-minded love is intrinsically better than all scientific insights combined. But I would say, not merely that this is questionable, but that it is altogether absurd. For any given act of love, valuable as it may be, is only a finite good. But every act of insight is also a finite good. If I keep adding this finite quantity to itself and continue long enough, sooner or later its sum will exceed any given finite quantity of good.* Plato and Aristotle, on the other

[37] [This note, "Two unique cases of preferability", may be found on page 90ff.]

* [Editor's note: The question whether insight is to be preferred

hand, were inclined to say that any given act of knowledge is superior, as such, to any particular act of virtue. But this view, too, is quite unjustified. I mention it only because the existence of opposing views on this question confirms that no criterion is available to us here. As is so often the case in the sphere of the psychological, measurement in the strict sense of the term is impossible.[38] We must say of intrinsic preferability what we said of simple goods—if we have no experience of the correctness that is involved, then, so far as our knowledge and practical concerns may go, it is non-existent.

*33* There are some who hold, in opposition to what experience makes evident to us, that pleasure is the only thing good in itself, that pleasure is *the* good. If this view were true, then, as Bentham urged, it would have the following advantage: since all goods would be homogeneous, we would be able to compare them quantitatively and thus determine their relative values.[39] Thus of any two pleasures, the more intensive would be better than the less intensive; a good of any given intensity would be equal in value to two goods each of which has half that intensity; and so everything would be clear and simple.

But only a moment's reflection is needed to shatter such illusory hopes. Is it really possible to find out whether one pleasure is twice as great as another? Gauss, who certainly knew something about measurement, has denied that this is pos-

[38] Compare my *Psychology from an Empirical Standpoint*, Book II, Chapter 4 (Vol. I).

[39] See Bentham's *Principles of Legislation*, Chapter 3, Section 1 (toward the end); Chapter 6, Section 2 (toward the end); and Chapters 8 and 9; in *Theory of Legislation*, trans. R. Hildreth (from the French trans. by E. Dumont); London, Trübner & Co., 1864.

to blind, instinctive pleasure is a different question. In a letter to me (November 1, 1913), Brentano said that, if we have the general concepts of pleasure and knowledge, then a preference that is experienced as being correct would dictate that it would be better to forego the pleasure than to forego the knowledge. In a similar vein, Aristotle and Mill said that no one would exchange the life of a human being for that of one of the lower animals, even if the latter choice were to ensure a lifetime of animal pleasure.]

sible.[40] A foot is divisible into twelve inches; but an intense joy is not divisible in the same sense into twelve less intensive joys. Consider how ridiculous it would be if someone said that the amount of pleasure he has in smoking a good cigar is such that, if it were multiplied by 127, or say by 1,077, it would be precisely equal to the amount of pleasure he has in listening to a symphony of Beethoven or in viewing one of Raphael's madonnas![41] This is enough, I think, to suggest the further difficulties involved in trying to compare the intensity of pleasure with that of pain.

*34* And so we see that experience gives us only very limited knowledge about those things that are better in themselves than others.

I can well understand how anyone who reflects on these matters

[40] See S. Rudolph Wagner, *Der Kampf um die Seele, vom Standpunkt der Wissenschaft* (Sendschreiben an Herrn Leibarzt Dr. Beneke in Oldenburg, Göttingen, 1857, p. 94n.): "Gauss said that the author [of a certain work on psychology] spoke of the absence of precise measurements in the case of psychological phenomena. Gauss himself said it would help considerably if there were even imprecise ones; for then we could at least make a beginning, but in fact we cannot. He felt that so far as psychological phenomena are concerned the *conditio sine qua non* of a mathematical treatment is absent; we do not know whether or to what extent an intensive quantity may be translated into an extensive one. To have such knowledge would be the first condition, and there are still others. On this occasion Gauss also spoke of the incorrectness of the usual definition of quantity as an *ens* which is capable of being increased or diminished; one should say instead that it is an *ens* which is capable of being divided into equal parts. . . ."

[41] Even if Fechner's psychophysical law were firmly established—actually, it has given rise to increasing doubt and opposition—it could be used only to measure the intensity of the content of certain sensuous presentations; it could not be used to measure the strength of emotions such as joy and sorrow. Some have tried to measure degree of feeling by reference to those involuntary movements and other externally visible changes that accompany the emotions. This is like trying to establish the exact day of the month by studying the weather. We can learn far more from our direct inner consciousness, however incomplete its testimony may be. At least we would be drawing from the spring itself; but in the other case, we are dealing with water that has been made impure by a great variety of external influences.

for the first time may fear that the limitations of this knowledge will make for extraordinary difficulties in practice. But if we proceed with care and make the most efficient use of that knowledge that we do have, we will find, fortunately, that even the most glaring of these limitations turn out in practice to be harmless.

*35* Our observations about the different cases of preference that are experienced as being correct have this important consequence: the sphere of the highest practical good is the whole area that is affected by our rational activities insofar as anything good can be brought about within it. Thus one must consider not only oneself, but also one's family, the city, the state, every living thing upon the earth, and one must consider not only the immediate present but also the distant future. All this follows from the principle of the summation of good. To further the good throughout this great whole so far as possible—this is clearly the correct end in life, and all our actions should be centred around it. It is the one supreme imperative upon which all the others depend.[42] It is thus a duty to give of oneself and even on occasion to sacrifice oneself. Any given good, whether in ourselves or in others, is to be loved in proportion to its value and it is to be loved equally wherever it may be found. Envy, jealousy, and malice are ruled out.[43]

[42] [This note, "On the charge of excessive rigorism", may be found on page 92ff.]

[43] But the commandment to love one's neighbour as oneself does not mean that we are to extend to all others the same active concern we have for ourselves. Instead of promoting the general good, following such a maxim would be prejudicial to it. The possibilities we have for promoting our own good are vastly different from the possibilities that we have for promoting the good of others. Similarly, we can help, or harm, some people much more than others. If there are people on Mars, we ought to wish them well, but it is not our duty to work for their good in the way in which we ought to work for ourselves and our fellow men upon the earth.

It is in this connection that we should understand the precept to be found in every system of morality: "Take thought first for oneself"; "γνῶθι σαυτόν"; "*Kehre vor der eigenen Türe!* [Sweep your own doorstep]." The obligation to look first toward the welfare of wife, child, and country is generally recognized. The maxim, "Take no thought for the morrow", in the only sense in which it really offers

*36* All narrower goods are to be subordinated to the good of this very broad realm. And so, on the basis of utilitarian considerations, we may now bring some clarity into the area that was previously obscure; for we are now in a position to say something more positive about the standard that ought to be applicable to any particular choice.* Even if there is no way of comparing the intrinsic value of acts of insight, say, with acts of high-minded love, it is clear, at least, that neither type of act is to be entirely neglected for the sake of the other. If one person had complete knowledge but felt no exalted love, and another felt the love but did not have the knowledge, neither would be able to put his gifts to the service of the larger collective good. From this point of view, it is clear that we should try to realize and harmonize all our noblest capacities.[44]

*37* Now that we have been able to see how so many duties toward the highest practical good arise, let us turn to the source

[44] We may be more disturbed, however, by the fact that it is often impossible to measure the remote consequences of our actions. But this type of uncertainty need not discourage us, if we really do love what is best on the whole. Of those possible consequences which are equally unknown, any one has as many chances in its favour as any of the others. According to the law of large numbers, results will balance out in the long run. Hence if we choose a good that we are sure of, then a plus will remain on the side of the good and our choice will be justified, just as it would be if it were to stand alone. We mentioned another type of uncertainty in the lecture (at the end of section 27)—the uncertainty arising out of the possibility that some good things may not be experienced by us as good. Similar considerations show that this type of uncertainty need not disturb us either.

* [Editor's note: Since the time of Kant, the term "utilitarian" has had an unfortunate connotation in Germany. The realm of value toward which, according to Brentano, we should endeavour to make ourselves as useful as possible is not restricted, of course, to pleasure or to oneself.]

---

wise counsel, follows from the same precept. But it does *not* mean that my future happiness should be of less value to me than the happiness of the present moment.

These considerations also indicate that there is no justification for the communistic doctrines which some have tried to deduce, much too rashly, from the lofty principles of universal brotherhood.

of our legal duties. One indispensable condition for bringing about the highest practical good is that we so live that a division of labour will be possible. It is morally necessary, therefore, that man live in society. From this it follows that each person should be to a certain extent restricted in his activities; otherwise he will bring more harm than good to those around him.[45] These restrictions can be made definite only by positive legislation (though much can be accomplished merely by the simple exercises of good sense), and they need the security and support of public authority.

And just as our natural insight requires and sanctions the existence of a positive law, it may also make particular demands which must be fulfilled if the legal order is to bestow upon us its full store of blessings.

Thus truth, which bears the highest crown, may sanction or refuse to sanction the products of positive legislation. It is from this sanction that they derive their true binding force.[46] The old sage of Ephesus observed, in one of his Sibyl-like utterances that are so full of meaning: "All human laws are nourished from the *one* divine law."[47]

[45] [This note, "Criticism of Ihering", may be found on page 93ff.]

[46] Reason may yet give provisional sanction to a law that is essentially bad and contrary to nature, no matter how much the law is to be condemned from a moral point of view and no matter how urgently it may require amendment. This has long been recognized and often been pointed out; see for example Bentham's *Theory of Legislation*. Socrates, who deemed himself worthy to be feasted in the Prytaneum, died for the sake of this conviction. The positive legal code, despite its defects, establishes a condition that is better than anarchy. Since each violation of the law threatens to weaken the force of law in general, it may well be that in order to preserve the existence of the legal order a rational man must occasionally pursue a course of action which would not otherwise deserve our approbation. This is a logical consequence of the relativity of secondary ethical rules— a matter which will be taken up later.

Errors in the prevailing moral codes must be looked upon in a similar way (this point is to be touched upon in the lecture).

But there are limits, and it is necessary to give heed to the sublime saying, "We owe greater obedience to God than to man".

[47] Heraclitus of Ephesus (500 B.C.), the first of the Greek philosophers from whose writings we have extensive fragments.

*38* In addition to those laws that set limits on our rights, every society has positive stipulations about the way in which the individual should act within his own sphere of rights, stipulations as to how he should make use of his own freedom and property. Public opinion approves diligence, generosity, and economy, each in its proper place, and disapproves indolence, greed, extravagance, and many other things. These prescriptions do not appear in any law books, but, as we may put it, they stand written within the hearts of the people. And they carry with them their own characteristic rewards and punishments—namely, the advantages and disadvantages, respectively, of good and of bad reputation. Thus we have, so to speak, a prevailing positive code of morality that supplements the prevailing positive code of law. This code of morality, like the code of law, may contain correct and incorrect precepts. If the precepts are to be truly binding, then, as we have seen, they must accord with what reason sees to be our duties toward the highest practical good.

And so we have found what we were looking for—the natural sanction for law and morality.

*39* I shall not pause to discuss the way in which this sanction makes itself felt. Everyone prefers to say "I am acting rightly", and not "I am acting wrongly". No one who is capable of recognizing what is better can be entirely indifferent to this fact when he comes to make a decision. For some, though not for others, it is a consideration of supreme importance. Natural endowments vary from one person to another, but much can be accomplished by means of education and self-guidance. Truth speaks, and whoever is of the truth hears its voice.

*40* We have seen that utilitarian considerations set the standard, so far as concerns the multiplicity of subordinate rules which nature engraves upon the tables of law. Just as we resort to different means in different situations, so, too, we should follow different precepts in different situations. Some of these may seem to conflict with others, but they do not conflict in fact, since they are intended to be applied to different types of situation. In *this* sense, it is correct to say that there is a kind of relativity in ethics.

Ihering has emphasized this type of relativity, but he is not, as he seems to think, one of the first to do so.[48] The doctrine was known in antiquity and Plato takes note of it in the *Republic*.[49] Aristotle emphasized it in the *Ethics* and made even more of it in the *Politics*.[50] It was acknowledged by the scholastics, and in modern times even Bentham, with his strong ethical and political convictions, has not denied it.[51] The fanatics of the French Revolution may have misconceived such relativity, but this is not true of the more circumspect among their compatriots. Laplace, for example, takes note of it in his *Essai philosophique sur les probabilités* and raises his voice in warning.[52]

The distinguished investigator who has disclosed to us the spirit of Roman law has given us much for which we should be grateful in *Der Zweck im Recht*. But he has obscured the true doctrine of ethical relativity by confounding it with a false doctrine of ethical relativism. According to the latter doctrine, *no* proposition in ethics has unexceptionable validity—not even the proposition that one ought to bring about the best within the widest area that one is capable of influencing. Ihering explicitly says that, in primitive times and for long periods afterwards, such a course of action would have been *immoral*, just as it is *moral* now. If we look back to the days of cannibalism, Ihering would have us sympathize with the cannibals instead of with those people who, in advance of their time, preached the universal love of one's neighbour.[53] These errors have been conclusively refuted, not only by philosophical reflection upon the principles of our knowledge of ethics, but also by the success of our Christian missionaries.

[48] Ihering, *Der Zweck im Recht*, Vol. II, p. 119 and elsewhere.

[49] Plato, *The Republic*, Book I, 331c.

[50] Aristotle, *Nichomachaean Ethics*, Book V, Chapter 10, 1137b 13; *Politics*, Books III and IV.

[51] See the Preliminary Discourse to Bentham's *Theory of Legislation*, as well as the "Essay on the influence of time and place upon the matter of legislation", in *Works of Jeremy Bentham*, ed. Bowring, London, William Tait, 1873; Vol. I, pp. 169–197.

[52] Pierre Simon Laplace, *Essai philosophique sur les probabilités*, Part II, Chapter 10 ("Application of the Calculus of Probabilities to the Moral Sciences").

[53] Cf. his article in *Allgem, Juristenzeitung*, Seventh Year, p. 171, and *Zweck im Recht*, Vol. II, pp. 118 and 122ff.

*41* We have now reached the end of the road leading to the goal we had set before us. The road took us through strange and unfamiliar territory. But the results we have finally attained seem like old acquaintances. In saying that love of one's neighbour and self-sacrifice for one's country and for mankind are duties, we are merely repeating what is proclaimed all around us. A more detailed investigation would also show that deceit, treachery, murder, lasciviousness, along with countless other such things that are held to be morally reprehensible, are also to be condemned as being either unjust or immoral on the basis of the principle of moral knowledge that we have set forth.*

And so we find ourselves returning to familiar territory, as though we had returned from a distant voyage and could see at last the outlines of our homeland and the smoke rising from our own chimney.

*42* We have a right to take pleasure in the familiarity of what we have found. The indubitable clarity with which everything follows is a good indication of the success of our undertaking. For the manner in which each step follows from the previous one is the most essential aspect of what we have said. Otherwise what advantage would the present inquiry have over any other? Even Kant, whose conception of our knowledge of right and wrong is very different from ours, arrived eventually at the most familiar views. But what we miss in his work is strict logical coherence. Beneke has shown that the Categorical Imperative, as Kant conceived it, may be used to prove contradictory propositions about one and the same thing and therefore to prove everything and nothing.[54] If we find, all the same, that Kant keeps drawing correct conclusions, we may attribute this to the fact that he had held them all along. Similarly, if Hegel had not known independently that the sky was blue, he would never have been able to deduce it *a priori* by means of his

---

[54] The reference is to Kant's *Grundlegung zur Metaphysik der Sitten*; see note 15 ("Kant's Categorical Imperative").

* [Editor's note: See Appendix V ("Epicurus and the War"). It may be noted that Brentano took very seriously the importance of sexual ethics and contributed a preface to the German edition of A. Herzen's, *Wissenschaft und Sittlichkeit : ein Wort an die männliche Jugend*, a manual that had been widely distributed in Germany.]

dialectic. (He also managed to deduce that there are exactly seven planets, the number accepted in his day—a view falsified by later scientific discoveries.)

The causes of the phenomenon are thus easily understood.

*43* But there is another point that is puzzling. How does it happen that the prevailing public opinion about what is right and what is moral is in so many respects correct? If such a philosopher as Kant failed in the attempt to find the source of our knowledge of right and wrong, is it conceivable that ordinary people succeeded in drawing from this source? And if it is not, how does it happen that they have so often arrived at the proper conclusions without having the necessary premises? One cannot possibly explain the fact by saying that the correct view was established long ago.

But this difficulty, too, is easily resolved, We have only to reflect that much of what is present in our store of knowledge contributes toward the attainment of new knowledge without our being clearly conscious of the process.

One must not infer that in saying this I am subscribing to the celebrated "philosophy of the unconscious". I am referring only to certain familiar and indisputable facts. It is well known that men were able to reason correctly for thousands of years without having reflected upon the principles of valid reason and even without knowing anything about them. Indeed, when Plato first contemplated these principles, he was led to adopt the erroneous view that inference always involves a process of reminiscence.[55] He thought that what we perceive and experience on earth enables us to recall what we had learned in some pre-terrestrial life. Of course no one believes this now. But we continue to encounter erroneous theories about the source of our knowledge of the syllogism. Albert Lange, for example, thinks that this knowledge arises out of a combination of spatial intuition and the synthetic *a priori*. Alexander Bain, on the other hand, says it arises out of the fact that our experience up to the present shows that whenever any of the moods, Barbara, Celarent, and the others, have true premises, they also have true conclusions.[56]

[55] See, for example, Plato's *Meno*.

[56] Friedrich Albert Lange, *Logische Studien: ein Beitrag zur Neubegründung der formalen Logik und der Erkenntnislehre* (Iserlohn, 1887); and Alexander Bain, *Logic* (London, 1870), Part I, "Deduction", p. 159.

These are the crudest possible erors about the kind of insight that such knowledge really involves; but they did not prevent Plato, Lange, and Bain from reasoning just the way that other people do. Despite their failure to recognize the true principles of knowledge, their reasoning none the less has conformed to these principles.

But why go so far to find our examples? All we need to do is to question any ordinary person who makes a correct inference. If we ask him to tell us the premises upon which his inference was based, we are likely to find that he is unable to do so and that he will give us an entirely inaccurate account of the way in which he has actually reasoned. Or if we ask him to define some concept that is very familiar to him, he is likely to make the most glaring of errors, thus demonstrating once again that he cannot correctly describe his own processes of thought.

*44* The road to ethical knowledge may seem obscure to the layman and also to the philosopher. The process is complex and there are many different principles working together. One would expect that some effects of each of these principles would be discernible throughout the course of history. This fact will do even more to confirm the correct theory than does the general agreement with respect to final results.

And what a multitude of examples could be cited if only there were time! Who would refuse to look upon joy (so long as it is not joy in what is bad) as an evident good? Many writers on ethics have even said that the concept of pleasure and the concept of good are one and the same.[57] But there have been others who in opposition bore witness to the intrinsic value of an insight, and anyone who has not had his head turned by theories must agree with them. Some have even wished to exalt knowledge to the position of being the highest good, elevated above all others.[58] But they also see a certain intrinsic value in every act of virtue. And others have said that virtuous action is the highest good.[59]

[57] For example, Bentham and, in antiquity, Epicurus.
[58] For example, Plato and Aristotle and, following them, Thomas Aquinas.
[59] For example, the Stoics and, in the middle ages, the followers of Scotus.

On these points, then, there is sufficient confirmation for our views.

And let us also consider the principles of preference. Do we not see the principle of summation exemplified in the dictum that the measure of happiness should be taken to be life as a whole and not merely the passing moment?[60] And passing beyond the limits of the self, we see the same principle exemplified in Aristotle's observation that the happiness of a whole people is a higher end than the happiness of oneself.[61] We find the same thing, he said, in a work of art, or in an organism, or in a household: the part exists for the sake of the whole, and everything is subordinate to the good of the whole ("εἰς τὸ κοινόν").[62] He even applies the same principle to the whole creation. He asks: "Where are we to look for the good and the best, which is the ultimate end of all created things? Is it immanent or is it transcendent?" And he answers, "Both", saying that the transcendent end is the divine first cause which all things strive to emulate and that the immanent end is the whole world-order.[63] The Stoics give similar testimony to the principle of summation.[64] Indeed, the principle reappears in every attempt to construct a theodicy, from Plato to Leibniz and even later.[65]

[60] Even Epicurus does not deny this—despite the fact that it conflicts with the assertion of his referred to in Section 31.

[61] Aristotle, *Nicomachaean Ethics*, Book I, Chapter 2.

[62] Aristotle, *Metaphysics*, Book XII, Chapter 10.

[63] Aristotle, *Metaphysics*, Book XII, Chapter 10. [Editor's note: compare the discussion in Brentano's *Aristoteles und seine Weltanschauung* (Leipzig: Quelle & Meyer), 1911.]

[64] They appealed to it when they argued that the life of the person who devotes himself to practical affairs is superior to the theoretical life.

[65] Appeal to the principle of summation is also made whenever the notion of God is employed in the construction of an ethical theory based on egoism and eudaemonism; for example, in Locke, in Fechner's work on the highest good, and in Leibniz (see Adolph Trendelenburg, *Historische Beiträge*, Vol. II, p. 245). God loves each of his creatures and therefore—so the argument goes—he loves them in their totality more than he loves each of them individually; hence he approves and rewards the sacrifice of the individual for the sake of this totality, while disapproving and punishing misdeeds committed for selfish purposes.

The influence of the principle of summation also shows itself in

It also appears in the precepts of our popular religion. The commandment to love our neighbour as ourselves tells us that we should give equal weight to every good, whether it be found in ourselves or in others. And this means that the individual should subordinate his own interests to that of the collective whole, just as the Saviour—the ethical ideal of Christianity— sacrificed himself for the salvation of the world.*

The commandment, "Love God above all else", is also a particular application of the law of summation. (As Aristotle said, God rather than the world as a whole is what is to be called the best.)[66] For do we not think of God as though he were the epitome of everything that is good, but raised to an infinite degree?

And so the two commandments—to love our neighbour as ourselves and to love God above all else—turn out to be so closely related that it is no longer surprising also to hear that the one is "like unto the other". It is very important to note that the commandment to love our neighbour is neither subordinate to nor in any way derivative from the commandment to love God. According to the Christian, the commandment to love our neighbour is right not in virtue of the fact that God requires it; God requires it in virtue of the fact that it is naturally

[66] Aristotle, *Metaphysics*, Book XII, Chapter 10, 1075a.

* [Editor's note: See Brentano's posthumous, *Die Lehre Jesu und ihre bleibende Bedeutung*, ed., Alfred Kastil (Leipzig: Felix Meiner, 1921).]

---

the desire for immortality. Thus Helmholtz, in seeking to offer hope to those who have this desire, writes: "If our achievements can enrich the lives of our descendants . . . then the individual may face without fear the thought that the threat of his own consciousness will some day be broken. But even such great and independent spirits as Lessing and David Strauss could not reconcile themselves to the thought that all living things, and therefore the fruits of the work of all past generations, might some day be annihilated." (See his "*Über die Entstehung des Planetensystems*", a lecture given at Heidelberg and Cologne, 1871). He believes that, if it is ever shown scientifically that the earth will one day be incapable of supporting life, then the need for immortality will once again establish itself, and people will then feel compelled to look for something which will show that belief in it is acceptable.

right.[67] The two commandments are alike in that their correctness is revealed in the same way, with the same clarity, and, so to speak, by means of the same light of natural knowledge.

Perhaps we now have sufficient evidence of the influence of some of the principles we have emphasized. And so on the one hand we have a kind of corroboration of our theory; and on the other hand we are able to explain those puzzling anticipations of philosophical results that are to be found in ordinary life.

*45* We are not to suppose, however, that everything has now been settled. Even when concealed, the pure and exalted sources of knowledge that we have discussed send forth their product in great abundance. But there are also opinions regarding law and morality that are accepted by society and have the sanction of ethics which do not in fact arise from these sources. Many of them have arisen in a way that is quite unjustifiable from the point of view of logic. Investigation shows that many have their origin in certain lower impulses, in self-centred desires that then underwent a transformation. It is true, as so many utilitarians have emphasized, that egoism gives men an incentive to make themselves agreeable to others and that such conduct, continually practised, finally develops into a habit which is no longer referred back to its original purpose. This is primarily a result of the narrowness of our intellect, the so-called limits of consciousness which make us lose sight of our more distant ends when some more immediate question is at hand. Thus the blind force of habit may lead many people to have a certain selfless regard for the well-being of others. It is also true, as many have pointed out, that there have been powerful personalities throughout the course of history who were able to subjugate certain weaker individuals and transform them through habit into willing slaves. Ultimately in these poor slave-souls there comes to operate an

---

[67] This is the orthodox view of the great theologians, for example, Thomas Aquinas in the *Summa Theologica*. Only certain nominalists— for example, Robert Holcot—held that divine commands are completely arbitrary. See my *"Geschichte der kirchlichen Wissenschaften"*, in Volume II of Johann Adam Möhler's *Kirchengeschichte*, edited by P. B. Gams (Regensburg: G. J. Manz, 1867), pp. 526–84; I would also call the reader's attention to the list of typographical errors to be found in Volume III of that work (pp. 103–4).

αὐτὸς ἔφα with a blind though powerful force; they come to hear a compelling "You ought" just as though it were a revelation of nature about good and evil. When the individual violates the command, he is inwardly tormented, just as a well-trained dog would be. The tyrant is well-advised, in his own interests, to issue commands conducive to maintaining his horde. His subjects will learn to obey these commands as slavishly and habitually as they do any others. Concern for the whole society will then become a goal towards which every subject feels himself impelled as though by nature. And the tyrant himself, because of his concern for his possessions, will also form habits favouring the collective welfare. Indeed, like the miser who sacrificed himself in order to preserve his treasure, the tyrant may be ready to die for the sake of his people. Throughout this entire process, ethical principles exercise next to no influence. The compulsions and attitudes which arise in this way have no connection with the natural sanction for morality and no intrinsic ethical value. Yet consider what happens when one such tribe enters into relations with another and finds that here, too, considerations of friendliness begin to prove advantageous. The kind of training to which the people have been submitted will be certain sooner or later to lead to the acceptance of principles which accord with those that arise out of the true source of our knowledge of right and wrong.

*46* Consider now an analogous situation. Men and animals have the blind habit of expecting similar events to recur under similar circumstances. This habit, which is exercised in countless instances, very often coincides with what one would do if one were to act in accordance with an induction fully conforming to the principles of the probability calculus. Indeed the similarity of the results has sometimes led even people with a knowledge of psychology to assume that the habitual instinctive process is no different from the one illuminated by mathematical insight, despite the fact that the two processes are as different as night and day.[68] We should take care not to suppose, therefore, that the true ethical sanction exerts any influence upon the pseudo-ethical developments we have described.

[68] [This note, "Mill's Conception of the Evident", may be found on page 96ff.]

*47* Of course these lower processes have their use. As is often pointed out, nature does well to leave so much that pertains to our welfare to instinctive drives such as hunger and thirst instead of to our reason.[69]

I had earlier conceded to Ihering (perhaps the justification for the concession is now more clear) that there have been periods of history in which there was practically no trace of ethical thought or feeling. But even then much occurred which was a preparation for true virtue. Public law and order, for whatever motives they may originally have been established, were preconditions for the unfolding of our noblest capacities.

Under the influence of such training some passions were checked and some dispositions were implanted which made it easier for people to conform to the true moral law. Catiline's courage was not the true virtue of courage—if Aristotle was right in saying that the truly courageous man is the one who faces danger and death τοῦ καλοῦ ἕνεκαι; that is to say, "for the sake of the morally beautiful".[70] Augustine might have appealed to his case when he said: "Virtutes ethnicorum splendida vitia". Yet one cannot deny that if Catiline had been converted then the dispositions he had acquired would have made it easier for him also to take the greatest risks for the sake of what is good. It is in this way that the ground was laid for the reception of genuine ethical insights. These preparatory steps greatly encouraged those who, acquiring for the first time knowledge of right and wrong and hearing within themselves the voice of the natural sanction, were then impelled to make the truth known to others. This is what Aristotle meant when he said that not everyone can study ethics: anyone who is to learn about law and morality must first be disposed toward what is good. It is a waste of effort, he said, for anyone else to study the subject.[71]

Indeed, those pre-ethical, though not pre-historic, times rendered still other services to the knowledge of natural law and morality. The legal ordinances and customs then established approached so very closely to what ethics demands, for the reasons

[69] Compare Hume, *Enquiry concerning Human Understanding*, Section 5, Part 2.
[70] Aristotle, *Nicomachaean Ethics*, Book III, Chapter 7; compare the subtle discussion in Chapter 8 of the five kinds of false courage.
[71] Aristotle, *Nicomachaean Ethics*, Book I, Chapter 3.

already discussed, that the similarity has led many to the mistaken belief that there was a deep and thorough-going relationship between these ordinances and customs, on the one hand, and ethics on the other. The precepts which are thus made into law by blind impulse often coincide in content with those which would be established on the basis of a knowledge of the good. In these codified laws and customs there are rough drafts, so to speak, of laws that ethics itself could sanction. And they were all the more valuable because they were adapted to the special circumstances of the people, as utilitarian considerations would require. Comparison of different laws and customs makes this latter point clear, just as, long ago, it helped lead to the important recognition of the correct sense in which one may speak of the relativity of natural law and morality. If Aristotle had not made such comparisons, would he have succeeded as he did in keeping himself free from stereotyped and doctrinaire theories?

So much, then, in order to give the pre-ethical ages their due.

*48* Nevertheless, it was then night. But it was a night that heralded the coming day, a day which will witness the most significant dawn in the history of the world. The day is yet to come; the forces of light are still struggling against the powers of darkness. Genuine ethical motives are by no means the generally accepted standard, either in private or in public life. These forces—to use the language of the poet—are not yet strong enough to hold the world together. We may be thankful that nature keeps us going by means of hunger and love and all those other obscure drives and strivings which are capable of being developed from self-seeking desires.

*49* The jurist, then, must take account of these drives and strivings and of the psychological laws that govern them if he is to understand his times and work for what is good. And he must also take into account those precepts of natural law and natural morality which, as we have suggested, were not the first to have emerged in the history of the subject, but which, if we may hope for a complete realization of the ideal, will be the last.

Here, then, we have in all its diversity the intimate relationship which, as Leibniz had seen, jurisprudence and politics bear to philosophy.

Plato said that the state will never thrive until the true philosopher is king, or until kings are able to philosophize in the proper way. In our own times we might put the point better by saying that the many defects of our political system will not begin to be corrected until our students of law, instead of being deprived of what little stimulus they now have to inform themselves about philosophy, are given a philosophical training that is adequate to their noble calling.

# SUPPLEMENTARY NOTES

## On Kant's Categorical Imperative
### (Note 14 to page 11)

In the *Grundlegung zur Metaphysik der Sitten*, (*Foundations of Morals*)* Kant formulates his categorical imperative in these two ways: "Act only in accordance with that maxim which you can at the same time will should become a universal law"; and "Act as if the maxim of your action were to become by your will a universal law of nature" (IV, 421 in the Akademie edition). In the *Critique of Practical Reason*,* he says: "Act so that the maxim of your will can always at the same time hold good as a principle of universal legislation" (V, 31). In other words, as Kant himself puts it, act upon a maxim which is such that, if it were to become a universal law, it would not lead to contradictions and thus nullify itself. Consciousness of this fundamental imperative, according to Kant, is a fact of pure reason, which thereby proclaims itself to be legislative (sic volo sic jubeo). But Beneke has long since observed that this supposed consciousness is only a "poetic, psychological fiction". (See his *Grundlinien der Sittenlehre*, 1841, Vol. II, p. xviii; compare his *Grundlegung zur Physik der Sitten*, which is a counterpart to Kant's *Grundlegung zur Metaphysik der Sitten*.) There is probably no longer anyone of sound judgement who would disagree with Beneke on this point. It is noteworthy that even philosophers such as Mansel, who have the highest esteem for Kant, concede that the categorical imperative is a fiction and manifestly untenable.

And the categorical imperative has still another defect which is no less serious. Even if one were to accept it, one could not use it to deduce any ethical consequences. As Mill correctly observes (*Utilitarianism*, Chapter 1), the deductions Kant himself attempts to make fail "in an almost grotesque fashion". The following is

* [Translations of these works appear in *Critique of Practical Reason and other writings in Moral Philosophy*, ed. and trans. Lewis White Beck; University of Chicago Press, 1949.]

Kant's favourite example of the way in which the categorical imperative is to be applied; it is to be found in the *Grundlegung zur Metaphysik der Sitten* (IV, 722) as well as in the *Critique of Practical Reason*. If a person has been entrusted with some possession, without giving a receipt or any other acknowledgement, is it right for him to keep it for himself? Kant answers: "No!" For, he says, if the contrary maxim were to become a universal law, then no one would entrust anything to anyone without a receipt. In this case, Kant says, the law could not be put into effect since there would be no instances to which it applied, and therefore it would nullify itself.

It is easy to see that Kant's reasoning is invalid and in fact absurd. If in consequence of a law certain actions cease to be performed, the law *does* exert an influence. It is therefore still effective and it has in no way nullified itself. To see the absurdity of what Kant says, we have only to deal with the following question in an analogous way: "Should I give in to a man who tries to bribe me?" The answer would have to be this: "Yes!" For if the contrary maxim were to become a universal law, then people would no longer attempt bribery. Therefore the law could not be put into effect since there would be no instances to which it applied, and therefore it would nullify itself.

## Descartes' Classification of Psychological Phenomena
### (Note 21 to page 15)

Descartes writes in the third Meditation: "It is requisite that I should here divide my thoughts (all mental acts) into certain kinds. . . . Of my thoughts some are, so to speak, images of the things, and to these alone is the title 'idea' properly applied; examples are my thought of a man or of a chimera, of heaven, of an angel, or of God. But other thoughts possess other forms as well. For example, in willing, fearing, approving, denying, though I always perceive something as the subject of the action of my mind, yet by this action I always add something else to the idea which I have of that thing; and of the thoughts of this kind some are called *volitions* or *affections*, and others *judgements*."[1]

[1] Nunc autem ordo videtur exigere, ut prius omnes meas cogitationes in certa genera distribuam. . . . Quaedam ex his tanquam

Despite this clear statement, we find Windelband saying that, according to Descartes, to judge is to will.[2] What misled him is Descartes' treatment, in the fourth Meditation, of the influence of the will in the formation of our judgements. Scholastic philosophers—Suarez, for example—were already attributing too much to this influence, and Descartes himself exaggerates it to the point of considering every judgement, even those which are evident, as the product of an act of will. But it is one thing to *produce* the judgement and quite another thing to *be* that judgement. The view that judgement is a product of the act of will does appear in the passage cited above, and it is probably what led Descartes to assign judgement to the third place in his classification of psychological phenomena. And yet he can add, quite consistently, concerning such phenomena, "Some are called volitions and *others* are called judgements".

There are two passages in Descartes' later writings which are more likely to lead us astray. One of these appeared in the *Principles of Philosophy* (Part I, Principle 32), written three years after the *Meditations*, and the other three years after that, in the *Notae in Programma*.[3] It is strange that Windelband did not appeal to the passage from the *Principles*, instead of to the one in the *Meditations*, for the former could easily lead one to suppose that Descartes had changed his views. The passage reads: "All the modes of thinking that we observed in ourselves may be related to two general modes, the one of which consists in perception, or in the operation of the understanding, and the other in volition,

---

[2] *Strassburger Abhandlungen zur Philosophie* (1884), p. 171.

[3] "Notes directed against a Certain Programme, published in Belgium at the end of the year 1647, under the title 'An Explanation of the Human Mind or Rational Soul: What it is and What it May be'."

---

rerum imagines sunt, quibus solis proprie convenit ideae nomen, ut cum hominem, vel chimaeram, vel coelum, vel angelum, vel Deum cogito; aliae vero alias quasdam practerea formas habent, ut cum volo, cum timeo, cum affirmo, cum nego, semper quiden aliquam rem ut subjectum meae cogitationis apprehendo, sed aliquid etiam amplius quam istius rei similitudinem cogitatione complector; et ex his aliae voluntates sive affectus, aliae autem judicia appellantur. [English trans. from the *Philosophical Works of Descartes*, trans. E. S. Haldane and G. R. T. Ross, Vol. I, p. 159.]

or the operation of the will. Thus sense-perception, imagining, and conceiving things that are purely intelligible, are just different modes of perceiving; but desiring, holding in aversion, affirming, denying, doubting, all these are the different modes of willing."[4]

This passage, which could easily be taken to conflict with what Descartes says in the third Meditation, may tempt one to suppose that he has abandoned his threefold classification, thus giving up Scylla for Charybdis. Has he avoided the older mistake of confusing judgement and idea only now to confuse judgement and will? A closer examination will show that this is not the proper interpretation and that Descartes has made no such mistake. Let us note the following points. (1) There is not the slightest indication that Descartes was ever aware of abandoning the views he had expressed in the third Meditation. (2) Moreover, in 1647—three years after the publication of the *Meditations* and shortly before the conception of *Notae in Programma*— Descartes published his revised translation of the *Meditations*, and he made no change whatever in the crucial passage in the third Meditation.[5] (3) In the *Principles* (Part I, Principle 42), just after the passage we have cited, he says that all our errors depend upon the will, but far from saying that our errors are themselves acts of will, he says that there is no one who would err voluntarily ("there is no one who expressly desires to err"). And there is an even more decisive indication of the fact that he views our judgements not as inner acts of will comparable to our desires and aversions, but as only the effects of the acts of will. For he immediately adds: "There is a great deal of difference between willing to be deceived and willing to give one's assent

---

[4] Ordines modi cogitandi, quos in nobis experimur, ad duos generales referri possunt: Quorum unus est perceptio sive operatio intellectus; alius vero volitio sive operatio voluntatis. Nam sentire, imaginari et pure intelligere, sunt tantum diversi modi percipiendi; ut et cupere, aversari, affirmare, negare, dubitare sunt diversi modi volendi. [Trans. Haldane and Ross, Vol. I, p. 232.]

[5] Entre mes pensées quelques-unes sont comme les images des choses, et c'est à celles-là seules que convient proprement le nom d'idée; ... D'autres, outre cela, ont quelques autres formes; ... et de ce genre de pensées, les unes sont appelées volontés ou affections, et les autres jugements.

to opinions in which error is sometimes found." He says of will, not that *it* affirms or assents, in the way in which it desires, but rather that it *wills* assent. Just as he says, not that it is itself true, but that it desires the truth ("it is the very desire for knowing the truth which causes . . . judgement on things").[6]

There can be no doubt about Descartes' real view; in the respects concerned it did not undergo any change at all. But we do have to explain the fact that he did alter the way in which he expressed his views. I think the solution is clearly as follows. Although he recognized that will and judgement are two fundamentally different types of mental phenomenon, he also saw that they have one feature in common which distinguishes them both from ideas. In the passage from the third Meditation, he notes that both will and judgement *add* something to the ideas on which they are based. And in the fourth Meditation he refers to another common character: the will decides with respect to both—it can initiate and withhold, not only its own acts, but also the acts of judgement. It is this feature which seems to him to be all-important in the first part of the *Principles* (numbers 29 to 42), and thus he contrasts ideas, which he takes to be operations of the understanding ("operationes intellectus"), with both judgement and will, which he takes to be operations of the will ("operationes voluntatis"). In the *Notae in Programma*, he again describes the acts of both judgement and will as being determinations of the will. "When I saw that over and above perception, which is required as a basis for judgement, there must needs be affirmation, or negation, to constitute the form of the judgement, and that *it is frequently open to us to withhold our assent*, even if we perceive a thing, I referred the act of judging which consists in nothing but assent, i.e., affirmation or negation, not to the perception of the understanding, but to the determination of the will."[7] Indeed, he does not hesitate to say in the *Principles* that both

[6] Nemo est que velit falli . . . Sed longe aliud est velle falli, quam velle assentiri iis, in quibus contingit errorem reperiri . . . Veritatis assequendae cupiditas . . . efficit, ut . . . judicium ferant. [Trans. Haldane and Ross, Vol. I, pp. 235–6.]

[7] Ego enim, cum viderem, praeter perceptionem, quae praerequiritur ut judicemus, opus esse affirmatione vel negatione ad formam judicii constituendam, nobisque saepe esse liberum ut cohibeamus assensionem; etiamsi rem percipiamus, ipsum actum judicandi, qui non

of these "modes of thinking" are "modes of willing", but from the context it is clear that he wishes only to say that both fall within the *domain* of the will.

We find additional support for this explanation if we consider the scholastic terminology with which Descartes had been familiar in his youth. It was customary to designate as *actus voluntatis* not only the motion of the will itself, but also anything performed under the control of the will. Hence there were said to be two kinds of acts of will—*actus elicitus voluntatis*, the acts of the will itself, and *actus imperatus voluntatis*, the acts that are performed under the control of the will. In the same way Descartes includes under one category both the *actus elicitus* of the will and what, according to him, can only be an *actus imperatus* of the will. But his classification must not be taken to imply that the intentional relation is the same in the two cases.

This explanation is clear enough if we consider all sides of the matter; yet we find Spinoza anticipating Windelband's misconception of the Cartesian doctrine. (It is more likely that Spinoza was misled by the passage in the *Principles* than by the one which Windelband cites from the *Meditations*.) In Proposition 49 of the Second Book of the *Ethics*, Spinoza himself interprets affirmation and negation as being, in the strictest sense, "volitions of the mind" ("volitiones mentis"), and then, as a result of still further confusion, he abolishes the distinction between the class of ideas and that of acts of will. The thesis now reads, "Will and understanding are one and the same",[8] so that the threefold classification of Descartes and the twofold classification of Aristotle are both discarded altogether. Here, as usual, Spinoza has served only to corrupt the doctrines of his great teacher.

## In Defence of a Theory of Judgement
(Note 22 to page 15)

All states of consciousness fall into one or the other of three groups: (i) merely contemplating something, having the thing

[8] Voluntas et intellectus unum et idem sunt.

---

nisi in assensu, hoc est in affirmatione vel negatione consistit, non rettuli ad perceptionem intellectus sed ad determinationem voluntatis. [English trans. from Haldane and Ross, Vol. I, p. 446.]

IN DEFENCE OF A THEORY OF JUDGEMENT

before the mind [*Vorstellen*]; (ii) judging [*Urteilen*]; and (iii) feeling or having an emotion [*Gemütstätigkeiten*]. I do not wish to claim, however, that there is now general agreement on this point. After all, if we had to wait for universal agreement, we could not even be sure of the law of contradiction; and in the present case there are some old prejudices that are not easily given up. Nevertheless no one has found it possible to bring forward a single serious objection to this conception of psychological phenomena, and this fact itself is a significant confirmation.

There are some—for example Windelband—who concede that judging and mere having before the mind should not be thought of as constituting one and the same type of phenomenon, but who do contend that judging and the feelings of emotions should be classified together. They make the mistake that Hume made in his discussion of belief. The act of affirming is taken to be an instance of approval, or valuing or prizing, on the part of the feelings, and the act of denying is taken to be an instance of disapproval, a rejection on the part of the feelings.

There is some analogy, to be sure, but it is difficult to see how this confusion could be made. There are people who affirm the goodness of God and the wickedness of the devil—the being of Ormuzd and that of Ahriman—with the same degree of conviction, yet they value and prize the being of the one, while feeling nothing but aversion and repulsion towards that of the other. Or again: we love knowledge and we hate error; hence it is entirely proper that we approve those *judgements* which we hold to be correct—and every judgement we make, after all, is one that we hold to be correct. Judging is related to feeling, then, in that we do thus approve of the judgements we make. But why would one confuse the judgement, which we may thus be said to approve, with the activity or feeling which is the approval itself? It is as though a man who loves his wife and child and material possessions came to confuse these objects with the love that he feels for them. Compare again what I have just said [in Note 21] about Windelband's mistake in ascribing such a doctrine to Descartes. One might also compare Sigwart's note about Windelband, parts of which are very much to the point.[1] Perhaps I may be permitted to refer anyone who needs further grounds for

[1] Sigwart's *Logik*, 2nd edn., Book I, pp. 156ff.

distinguishing the second and third of these basic types of phenomena to my forthcoming *Deskriptive Psychologie*. This work,
which is almost completed, will be a further development, and
not just a continuation, of my *Psychologie vom empirischen Standpunkt*.*
I have just a few more remarks, in opposition to what Windelband has to say.

(1) He writes, on page 172, that according to me "love and
hate" is not an appropriate designation for this third class of
psychological phenomena; indeed, he attributes to me a quotation to this effect. But he is entirely mistaken and has made a
serious oversight—as he could verify for himself by re-reading
Vol. I, page 262, of my *Psychologie*.[2]

(2) On page 178, he says that, according to me, the only classification of judgements which pertains to the act of judging itself
is the classification according to *quality*; but this too is a mistake,
and one which is entirely unjustified. My own belief is just
the contrary; unlike Windelband, I believe that both the distinction
between assertoric and apodictic judgements and the distinction
between evident and blind judgements pertain to the act of
judgement itself, and also that these distinctions are of basic
importance. And I could cite still other distinctions—for example,
the distinction between simple and compound acts of judgement. For it is not possible to resolve every compound judgement into entirely simple elements. The same can be said of
certain compound concepts, as Aristotle saw. What is it to be red?
To be coloured red. What is it to be coloured? To have the
quality of being coloured. In each case the concept of the genus
is contained in that of the specific difference; the separability of
the one logical element from the other is thus one-sided. And
we find the same situation, I believe, with respect to certain
compound judgements. J. S. Mill said that to classify judgements as simple and complex would be like classifying horses as
single horses and teams of horses.[3] But he is quite wrong in ridi-

---

[2] [Second edition, Vol. II, p. 35ff.]

[3] J. S. Mill. *Logic*, Vol. I, Bk. I, Chap. 4, Sec. 3.

* [Editor's note: The *Deskriptive Psychologie* that Brentano here
announces exists only in the form of lecture notes. But see Volume II
of his *Psychology from an Empirical Standpoint*, as well as his *Vom
sinnlichen und noetischen Bewusstsein* (Leipzig: Felix Meiner, 1928).]

culing this traditional classification; for his argument would apply equally well to the distinction between simple and compound concepts.

(3) Still another mistake—which almost everyone has made and which I, too, made in the first volume of the *Psychologie*— is that of supposing that one's "degree of conviction", so-called, is a kind of intensity analogous to the intensity of pleasure and pain. Were Windelband to accuse me of *this* mistake, his accusation would be entirely just. Instead, however, he criticizes me because I say that the so-called intensity of conviction is only analogous to, and not the same as, the variety of intensity experienced in pleasure and pain, and because I say that the (supposed) intensity of conviction and the (real) intensity of feeling are not comparable with respect to magnitude. This is one of the consequences of what Windelband takes to be his improved theory of judgement!

If a man's belief that $2+1 = 3$ had a degree of conviction which was literally an intensity, consider how powerful it would be! And if, as Windelband would have it (p. 186), the belief were a *feeling* in the strict sense of the word, and not merely something bearing a certain analogy to feeling, consider the havoc and violence to which the nervous system would be submitted! Our doctors might well tell us that, for the sake of our health, we should avoid the study of mathematics. (Compare what J. H. Newman has to say about the so-called degree of conviction in *An Essay in Aid of a Grammar of Assent*—an interesting work which has received but little notice in Germany.)

(4) Windelband wonders how I could think that the word "is" has one and the same meaning in such sentences as "There is a God", "There is a human being", "There is a deprivation", "There is a possibility", and "There is something which is true" (p. 183). Referring to my *Von der mannigfachen Bedeutung des Seienden nach Aristoteles*, he finds it odd that anyone who writes on the manifold significance of being should fail to take account of this manifold significance himself (p. 184). I can only say that if Windelband cannot see what my theory of judgement obviously implies in this case, then he has not understood the theory at all. Aristotle, in treating this question, divides being (ὄν) in the sense of being a thing into different categories and into actuality (ὄν ἐνεργείᾳ), and potentiality (ὂν δυνάμει), but it never occurs to

him to do the same with "is" (ἔστιν), which transforms the expression of an idea into that of a judgement, or with what he calls being in the sense of the true (ὂν ὡς ἀληθές). No one would think of making such a distinction unless, like Herbart and so many after him, he had failed to distinguish the concept of being in the sense of the true, and being in the sense of being a thing. (Compare the following discussion of Sigwart's doctrine.)

(5) I have said above that there are simple and compound judgements, and that there are some compound judgements which cannot be resolved without remainder into judgements which are simple. We must consider this fact when we try to reduce to existential form those judgements which have a different linguistic formulation. For it is obvious that only simple judgements—those which are truly unitary—can be so reduced. It goes without saying that this qualification should be made, and therefore I did not mention it in the *Psychologie*. And if the qualification holds generally, it also holds for the categorical forms of traditional logic. The A, E, I, and O statements are interpreted by the formal logician as expressions of judgements which are strictly unitary, and therefore they can be reduced to existential form.[4] But such reduction is not possible when the ambiguity of our language allows us to use a single categorical statement to express a plurality of judgements.[5] An existential formula can be used to express a unitary categorical judgement which is equivalent to the compound judgement, but it cannot adequately express this compound judgement itself.

Windelband should have taken these facts into consideration when, on page 184, he asks whether the statement "The rose is a flower" can be put into existential form. He is quite right in saying that the statement cannot be formulated as "There is no rose which is not a flower", but he is mistaken in thinking that I would disagree. I have never said—in the passage cited or anywhere else—that it *could* be so expressed. "The rose is a flower" cannot be expressed in *this* way, nor can it be expressed in the the way in which Windelband and so many others would have it. For the statement expresses *two* judgements, one of which consists in the acceptance or affirmation of the subject of the judgement—which could be "the rose", in the usual sense of

[4] See my *Psychologie*, Vol. II, pp. 53ff.
[5] See my *Psychologie*, Vol. II, p. 183 and pp. 158ff., esp. pp. 164ff.

ON EXISTENTIAL AND NEGATIVE JUDGEMENTS

this word, or "that which is called a rose", or "that which is understood as a rose". But, as we have remarked above, there are statements of the form "All A are B" which do *not* express any judgement accepting or affirming the subject. Unfortunately this point has also been overlooked by Land— the only one of my critics who has understood what Windelband has called my "mysterious" suggestions for reforming elementary logic; he has seen their necessary connection with the principle which I have used and he has been able to derive them correctly from this principle.*

Let me call attention finally to a certain curio which Steinthal has recently provided for us, in his *Zeitschrift fur Völkerpsychologie* (Vol. xviii, p. 175). Here I am amazed to read: "Brentano completely separates judgements from ideas and from thinking [!], and classifies judgements, as acts of acceptance or rejection, with love and hate [!!]—a confusion which is instantly dispelled, if one interprets any such judgement [?] as being rather a matter of taking an aesthetic [!] stand or position." Probably Steinthal read only Windelband's review, and did not look at my *Psychologie* itself. But he must have read the review in such a cursory fashion that perhaps he will appreciate my forwarding his lines to Windelband for correction.

## On Existential and Negative Judgements
(Note 23 to page 16)

Sigwart has published a monograph, *Die Impersonalien*, attacking Miklosich.[1] Marty wrote a penetrating criticism of the monograph in the *Vierteljahrsschrift für wissenschaftliche Philosophie*; he had previously criticized the relevant portions of Sigwart's

[1] Franz Miklosich, *Subjektlose Sätze*, Second Edition (Vienna: Braumüller, 1883). If the reader wishes to acquaint himself with this valuable work, I may suggest that he read the notice of it I prepared for the *Wiener Abendpost*. Through a misunderstanding it was published as a *feuilleton* in the *Wiener Zeitung*, where no one would think of looking for it, and so I include it in the present book.
* See J. P. N. Land, "On a supposed Improvement in Formal Logic", *Abhandlungen der Königl. Niederländischen Akademie der Wissenshaften*, 1876.

*Logik.** Quite unreasonably, Sigwart seems to have been considerably annoyed. "Il se fache", as the French would say, "donc il a tort". Steinthal burns thick clouds of incense on behalf of Sigwart in his *Zeitschrift* (Vol. xviii, pp. 170ff.), and in the foreword to the fourth edition of his own *Ursprung der Sprache* we find him approving what any true friend of the deserving Sigwart can only regret; yet even Steinthal admits that Sigwart's view is mistaken in its essentials. After the high praise with which he begins his review, we end up feeling somewhat disillusioned. Steinthal (pp. 177–180) rejects the grammatical implications of Sigwart's theory; hence the only real achievement Steinthal attributes to the monograph must be its contributions to psychology. But psychology is not the area in which Steinthal's judgement is authoritative. If it were, one would have to be serious even about the following remark: "On hearing the lines 'Da bückt sich's hinunter mit liebendem Blick' (from Schiller's *Taucher*), no one can fail to think of the daughter of the king. It is not she who comes before the mind, however; it is only a subjectless bow or curtsey. And now I feel myself even more with her. According to my [i.e., Steinthal's] psychology, the idea of the king's daughter hovers in the background, but does not enter consciousness." The wise man knows when he has had enough.

## I

The limitations of Sigwart's psychological theory become glaringly apparent when he tries to come to terms with the concept "existence". Aristotle realized that this is a concept we acquire through reflection upon the affirmative judgement.[2]

[2] The concepts of existence and non-existence are correlatives to the concepts of the truth of (simple) affirmative and negative judgements. The judgement is correlative with that which is judged; the affirmative judgement with that which is judged affirmatively, the negative judgement with that which is judged negatively. So, too, the correctness of the affirmative judgement is correlated with the existence of that which is affirmatively judged, and that of the negative judgement with the non-existence of that which is negatively judged. We may say either that an affirmative judgement is true or

* [Editor's note: See Anton Marty, *Gesammelte Schriften* (Halle: May Niemeyer, 1918), Vol. II, Section 1.]

But Sigwart, like most modern logicians, fails to follow the lead of Aristotle on this point. He does not say that the existent comprises everything of which the affirmative judgement is true. Instead of this, he goes into a lengthy discussion of the concept of being and the existential proposition. But Sigwart is on the wrong track altogether, and his views on these questions—which he sets forth again in the second edition of his *Logik* (pp. 88–95)—do not throw light on anything at all.

"To be", according to Sigwart, expresses a relation (pp. 88, 95). What kind of a relation? At first consideration (p. 92), one might suppose it to be a "relation to me as one who is thinking". But this will not do, for the existential proposition is said to assert precisely the fact that "that which has being exists apart from its relation to me or to any other thinking being". But if the relation in question is not "a relation to me as one who is thinking", what could it be? We do not find out until page 94. Here we are told that the relation is (to be sure, Sigwart adds: "to begin with") an "agreement of the thing thought about with a possible perception"; he also says it is an "identity" (p. 94) of the thing thought about with something "perceivable", or with "something which can be perceived by me" (p. 90, note).

We can see at once that his concept of existence is too narrow. For much of what exists cannot be perceived; for example, a past and a future, an empty space, any kind of deprivation, a possibility, an impossibility, and so on. It is not surprising,

---

that its object is existent; *in both cases we are saying precisely the same thing.* Similarly for saying that a negative judgement is true, and saying that its object is non-existent. We may say that, for every (simple) affirmative judgement, either it or the corresponding negative judgement is true; and we may express precisely the same logical principle by saying that, for every such affirmative judgement, either its object is existent or its object is non-existent.

The assertion of the truth of the judgement, that there is a learned man, is thus correlative to the assertion of the existence of its object, viz., a learned man. The assertion of the truth of the judgement, that no stone is alive, is similarly correlative to the assertion of the non-existence of its object, viz., a living stone. Correlative assertions, here as elsewhere, are inseparable. Compare such correlatives as "*A* is greater than *B*" and "*B* is less than *A*", or "*A* produces *B*" and "*B* is produced by *A*".

therefore, that Sigwart himself makes an effort to widen his concept. But what he does is very difficult for me to understand. First, he seems to say that, in order for a thing to be counted as existing, the thing need not be capable of being perceived by me; it is necessary only that it be capable of being perceived by someone or other. At least this seems to be what he means when, after saying that existence is an agreement between the thing thought about and a possible perception, he goes on to say: "That which exists bears *this relation* not only to me but also to everything else that has being." Surely Sigwart does not mean to say that everything that exists is capable of perceiving everything. Perhaps he means only that everything that exists stands in the relation of existence to every other being, in which case his empty-sounding phrase might be taken to mean that to say something exists is to attribute to it the capacity of acting and being acted upon. (Thus he tells us that "what exists . . . stands in causal relations to the rest of the world", and, in a footnote on page 91, that the existent is that which "can exercise effects upon me and others".) By the time we reach the end, however, there is some ground for supposing that what Sigwart wants to say is something like this: the existent is that which can be perceived or that which can be inferred as capable of being perceived. For he adds that "in consequence [i.e., in consequence of this causal relation] a merely *inferred* existence may be ascribed to that which is *capable of being perceived*".

But it is plain to see that these various assertions are equally unacceptable.

For (1) "to infer the existence of something" does not mean the same as "to infer that it is capable of being perceived". Thus if we were warranted in inferring, say, the existence of atoms and empty spaces, we would not thereby become warranted in inferring that these things could be perceived by us or by any other creature. Or if we were to infer that God exists, but resist the temptation to "enliven" our concept anthropomorphically, we would not therefore suppose that God can be perceived by any of his creatures or even by himself.

(2) Given Sigwart's point of view, it would be self-contradictory for a person to say: "I am convinced that there are many things the existence of which can never be perceived or even inferred by anyone." For he would be saying only: "I am con-

vinced that many of the things which can be perceived, or which can be inferred to be perceivable, can never be perceived or even inferred by anyone." Who could fail to see that Sigwart has left the true concept of existence far behind!

(3) Or did Sigwart, in the passage cited, intend to extend his concept of existence in such a way that what exists could be said to be that which is either capable of being perceived, or that which can be inferred from that which is capable of being perceived, or that which stands in some sort of causal relation to that which is capable of being perceived? If so, we would have to reply that the concept is still too narrow—if such a monstrous determination of the concept of existence requires refutation. Suppose I say, for example: "Perhaps there is an empty space, but this can never be known with certainty." I would be saying that perhaps empty space exists, but I would be denying that it is capable of being perceived, or that it can be inferred from what is capable of being perceived. An empty space (since it is not itself a thing) cannot be related as cause or effect to anything that is capable of being perceived. And so Sigwart's view, once again, would transform a perfectly sensible assertion into one that is utter nonsense.

The extent of Sigwart's error, in his analysis of the concept of existence, may be indicated very simply by the following: no real centaur exists; but a *contemplated* or *thought-about* centaur [*ein vorgestellter Zentaure*] does exist, and indeed it exists as often as I think of it. If there is anyone who fails to see, in this instance, the distinction between the ὄν ὡς ἀληθές (*being* in the sense of the true or of the existing) and the ὄν in the sense of the real (thing-hood), I am afraid that he would be unable to appreciate the abundance of other illustrations to which we might also appeal.

But let us also consider the following. According to Sigwart, knowledge of the existence of anything must consist in the knowledge of an agreement between the content of an idea and something else. I do not clearly understand what this something else is, so let us call it simply $x$. What, now, is required in order to know that one thing is in agreement with another thing? Obviously, a knowledge of everything which is necessary in order for there to be such an agreement. It is necessary, first, that there be the one thing, secondly that there be the other thing, and thirdly that there be a relation of identity holding between them; for that which is not can neither be the same as nor be different from that which is. But the knowledge of the first of these three items is itself already the knowledge of an existence. Hence the knowledge of the other two is no longer required in order for us to have any knowledge of existence; and therefore Sigwart's theory leads to a contradiction. (Compare what is said here with Sigwart's polemic against my *Psychologie*, Book II, Chapter 7, [Vol. I] in his *Die Impersonalien*, pp. 5off., and his *Logik*, 2nd ed., Vol. I, pp. 89ff. See also Marty's polemic against Sigwart in the articles, "Über subjektlose Sätze", in the *Vierteljahrsschrift für wissenschaftliche Philosophie*, Vol. VIII.)*

## II

If Sigwart misconceives the nature of judgement in general, then we can hardly expect that he will understand the nature of the negative judgement in particular. And indeed he goes so far astray that he refuses to regard the negative judgement as being a species of judgement on an equal footing alongside the positive or affirmative judgement. No negative judgement is direct, he says; its object is always some other judgement or an attempt to make some other judgement (*Logik*, 2nd edn., Vol. I, p. 150).

With this assertion, Sigwart contradicts certain important psychological theses which I have defended. It seems appropriate, therefore, for me to counter his attack. I wish to show three things. (1) Sigwart's own theory is without adequate foundation. (2) It leads to hopeless confusion: for Sigwart's affirmative

* I had already written my critique of Sigwart's concept of existence when I came across a certain note in his *Logik*, 2nd edn., Vol. I, p. 390. The note does not make it necessary to change anything, but I shall add it here for purposes of comparison. " 'Being' in general", Sigwart says, "cannot be regarded as a true generic concept which applies to particular individuals; conceptually regarded it is only a common name. Since 'being' is for us a relational predicate, it cannot be a common characteristic; if it were, it would have to be shown that the ground of this predicate lies in a determination common to the concept of everything that there is." I am afraid that this passage will no more enlighten my readers about Sigwart's concept of existence than it did me; it may help to show, however, why all my efforts to understand his concept have been in vain.

judgement is negative; his negative judgement—if it *is* a judgement and not merely the lack of a judgement—is positive; and his positive judgement actually involves a negative judgement. Such confusions are compounded. Finally (3) I wish to show the genesis of Sigwart's mistake; Sigwart's detailed discussions make it possible to do this.

(1) The first question that arises in the face of such a novel and outlandish assertion is: What kind of basis does it have? Sigwart emphasizes above all else (p. 150) that a negative judgement would have no meaning unless it were preceded by the thought of the positive attribution of a predicate. But what is this assertion supposed to mean? Unless it is a simple *petitio principii*, it tells us only that a connection of ideas must have preceded the negative judgement. If we suppose for the moment that the latter proposition is true (though I have shown in my *Psychologie* that it is not true), then the thesis in question would still not be established. For Sigwart himself (p. 89n. and elsewhere) realizes that no such "subjective connection of ideas" constitutes a judgement; there must be in addition (he would say) a certain feeling of compulsion.

Sigwart subsequently formulates another argument (p. 151), but I find it equally difficult to follow. He notes, quite correctly, that there are countless predicates which we have the right to deny of any given thing; and he adds, equally correctly, that we do not in fact make all of these negative judgements. But now —what are we to infer from these premises? That the fact that a given negative judgement is justified is not itself sufficient to account for the fact that the judgement is made? This, of course, we may admit without pause. But what Sigwart infers is quite different. A necessary condition for making a negative judgement, he says, is that we first attempt to make the corresponding positive judgement; hence if we do not make the attempt at the positive judgement, we do not make the negative judgement. This is a bold leap indeed, which *my* logic, at least, is unable to follow. What if we were now to ask, "And why is it that all the corresponding positive judgements are not attempted?" Sigwart's examples ("This stone reads, writes, sings, composes verses", "Justice is blue, green, heptagonal, moves in circles") would require the following answer: the reason that we do not attempt the positive judgement is that we have already made the negative judgement, and found it to be evident and certain. This is what would best explain why there is no "danger" of "anyone wanting to attribute such predicates to the stone or to justice". Another acceptable explanation of why we do not attempt all the relevant positive judgements would be that our consciousness, after all, has its limitations. But if this is Sigwart's line, why didn't he appeal directly to this fact earlier in his discussion? He says himself that there is an "unlimited number" of possible negative judgements.

Sigwart makes still another curious mistake (as Marty has already noted). Affirmative judgements, he says, differ from negative judgements in that "only a finite number of predicates can be affirmed of any subject". How so? Aren't we justified in saying, for example, that a whole hour is greater than a half an hour, greater than a third of an hour, greater than a fourth of an hour, and so on, *ad infinitum*? If now I do not in fact make each one of these judgements, there must be a good reason. After all, the limitations of consciousness would hardly permit it. But these same considerations may be applied equally well to negative judgements.

We find a third argument somewhat later on. We may treat it briefly here, for I have already refuted it in my *Psychologie* (Book II, Chapter 7, Section 5). Sigwart reasons as follows (p. 155f.): suppose the negative judgement is direct and, as a species of judgement, co-ordinate with the affirmative judgement; then, if the affirmation of the subject is involved in an affirmative categorical proposition, it follows that the denial of the subject is involved in a negative categorical proposition; but it is not. The latter observation is correct. (The denial of the subject need not be involved in the affirmation of a negative proposition.) But the observation that precedes it (viz., if one thinks that the affirmation of the subject is involved in an affirmative categorical proposition, one should also think that the denial of the subject is involved in a negative proposition) is entirely untenable and, indeed, self-contradictory. Precisely because of the fact that the existence of a whole involves the existence of each of its parts, all that is needed, if a given whole is *not* to exist, is that at least one of its parts be lacking.

There is, finally, a linguistic consideration which Sigwart believes will confirm his view. He says that we symbolize a negative judgement by adding a certain complication to the way in which we symbolize an affirmative judgement; we add the word "not" to the copula. To evaluate this, let us for a moment consider the emotions. Sigwart agrees with me, and with everyone else, that pleasures and displeasure, rejoicing and sorrowing, loving and hating, and the like are co-ordinate with each other. Yet we have a large group of expressions which are such that the names for feelings of disinclination are dependent upon the names for feelings of inclination. Thus we have: "inclination" and "disinclination"; "pleasure" and "displeasure"; "fortunate" and "unfortunate"; "happy" and "unhappy"; "agreeable" and "disagreeable"; and (in German) *"lieb"* and *"unlieb"*, *"schön"* and *"unschön"*, and even *"ungut"*. I believe that the psychologist will not find this fact difficult to explain, despite the fact that we have here two co-ordinate species of emotive phenomena. But if this is so, why should there be a difficulty in reconciling the corresponding fact, about the way in which negative judgements are expressed, with the fact that there are two co-ordinate species of intellectual phenomena?

If a thinker of Sigwart's calibre must take refuge in this type of argument to defend an important and unorthodox doctrine, then his case must be very poor indeed!

(2) There is no tenable basis, then, for Sigwart's theory of the negative judgement. And this is as it should be. One should not expect to be able to demonstrate a theory which seems to plunge everything into the greatest possible confusion.

Sigwart now finds himself compelled to distinguish a *positive* judgement and an *affirmative* judgement. And he goes on to say (this new terminology is dumbfounding!) that the *affirmative* judgement is, strictly speaking, a negative judgement! In his own words: "The original and primordial judgement should not be called affirmative; it would be better to say that it is a positive judgement. The simple assertion, that *A* is *B*, should be called *affirmative* only in opposition to a negative judgement and only *insofar* as it may be said to *reject* the possibility of a negation (p. 150)." Insofar as it "rejects"? What can this mean other than "insofar as it *denies*"? And so it really is true that, given this strange new use of words, only denials are to be called affirmations! But all this—especially if one is also going to say that the assertion, *A* is *B*, is sometimes such a denial (compare the words cited above)—multiplies linguistic confusion beyond necessity and beyond endurance.

Not only does the affirmative judgement turn out to be strictly negative, on Sigwart's account; we also find, paradoxical as it may seem, that his *negative* judgement, when closely examined, is a *positive* judgement. He does protest against the view of Hobbes and others, according to which negative judgements are really positive judgements with negative predicates. On *his* view, however, they have to be positive judgements with positive predicates; for he says that the subject of a negative judgement is always a judgement and that its predicate is the concept "invalid". Thus he says (p. 160n.) that negation serves to cancel out a supposition and to reject it as invalid (*spreche ihr die Gültigkeit ab*); these words would suggest that Sigwart does suppose that there is a special function of rejecting which is contrary to that of affirming. But no; according to him (see p. 153) there is no such thing as a negative copula. How on earth are we to interpret his "rejection", then? Could it be the simple "cessation" of the positive judgement about the corresponding subject-matter—and thus (on Sigwart's view) the disappearance of the feeling of compulsion which had previously existed along with a joining of concepts? This could not possibly be; for if the feeling of compulsion disappears, then, on Sigwart's view, there remains only a joining of ideas without any affirmation or negation. Consider how often it happens that something previously certain becomes uncertain—without our therefore rejecting or denying it. What is it, then, to reject or deny? Could we say that just as, for Sigwart, affirmation is a feeling of being compelled to posit, denial or negation is a feeling of being compelled to cancel out? In this case we should have to say that, whenever we make a negative judgement, we have found ourselves frustrated in a previous attempt to make the corresponding positive judgement. But he who finds simply that there is no ground for the positive judgement is in a similar state of mind; whoever could bring himself to believe a proposition he holds to be totally groundless? Certainly, such an attempt would be inconceivable on Sigwart's own definition of judgement; it would always end in failure. And so we have not yet been able to get the negative judgement clearly before us. If there is no negative copula, then rejection or denial would have to be a matter of attributing the predicate "false" to something, or, in Sigwart's terms, a matter of inserting this predicate into a judgement having the judgement in question as its subject. But this "false" cannot be said simply to mean the same as "not true". For we can say of countless things that they are "not true", where it would hardly be appropriate to say of them that they are "false". If judgements are the only things that can be said to be true, then "not true" applies to everything that is not a judgement; but "false" does not at all apply to everything that is not a judgement. Thus "false" must be conceived as a positive predicate. Hence, given Sigwart's point of view, which is inherently wrong, just as we must say that negation or denial is something other than mere failure to be convinced, we must say that every negative judgement is a positive judgement with a positive predicate. And thus we have a paradox which is even more striking than the first one we encountered.

But there is a third paradox, which serves to make the confusion complete. If we consider the way in which Sigwart conceives the nature of judgement in general, we can easily see that his simple positive judgement involves, again, a negative judgement. According to him, every judgement involves, not only a certain connection of ideas, but also a consciousness of the necessity of our putting them together and of the impossibility of the opposite (see in particular p. 102), and, indeed, it involves the consciousness of such a necessity and impossibility for every thinking being (pp. 102, 107)—which, incidentally, is just as much mistaken as is Sigwart's whole concept of the nature of judgement. Because of this characteristic, then, Sigwart says that *every* judgement without exception is apodictic; there is no valid distinction, according to him (see pp. 229ff.), between assertoric and apodictic judgements. I would ask, therefore: Do we not have here that which obviously involves a negative judgement? Otherwise what sense could we give to Sigwart's "consciousness of the impossibility of the opposite"? And there is still more! I have already shown in my *Psychologie* [Bk. II, Chap. VII (p. 59 in Vol. II)] that every universal judgement is negative; for to be convinced of universality is no more nor less than to be convinced that there is no exception. Without this latter negation, no accumulation of positive assertions, however extensive, would be sufficient to constitute a belief in universality. Hence when Sigwart says that every judgement involves the awareness that such-and-such a way of thinking must be universal, we have additional confirmation for our contention that, according to Sigwart's theory of judgement, even the simplest positive judgement has to involve a negative judgement. Are we really supposed to believe, then, that the negative judgement shows up relatively late (as we are told on pp. 159ff.) and that, on the basis of these and other considerations, the negative judgement should be thought unworthy of being placed on an equal footing with the positive judgement as being an independent species of judgement? The more one considers Sigwart's views the clearer it becomes that they do involve the implications developed here; surely Sigwart would never have maintained such things had he thought them through. There are passages, of course, in which he contradicts one or another of these theses which I have shown his views to imply. But what else are we to expect when everything is in such great confusion and when the attempt to clear up things serves only to uncover a multiplicity of contradictions?

(3) We have, then, a highly respected logician, misconceiving the nature of judgement and then becoming entangled in hopeless confusion with respect to a relatively simple question. What is the origin of the error? The *proton pseudos* consists of a mistake which has been handed down from the older logic; it is the mistake of supposing that a relation between two ideas is a part of the essence of a judgement. Aristotle had described the relation as being one of combining or separating (σύνθεσις καὶ διαίρεσις); he realized, however, that the terminology is not entirely appropriate, and he noted that there is a sense in which both relations could be said to be a matter of combining (σύνθεσις); see *De Anima*, Bk. III, chap. 6. Scholastic logic and modern logic have retained the two terms "combining" and "separating", but in grammar both relations are called "combining" and the symbol for combining is called the "copula". Now Sigwart takes these expressions "combining" and "separating" literally. Hence a negative copula appears to him to be a contradiction (see p. 153); and the negative judgement is said to presuppose a positive judgement. For how can we separate any two things unless they have first been combined? Thus we find that, according to Sigwart (p. 150 and the passages cited above), it makes no sense to speak of a negative judgement which does not presuppose a positive judgement. The consequence is that

all the efforts of this distinguished thinker turn out to be in vain; the negative judgement is no longer even comprehensible. There is a note, beginning on p. 150, in which Sigwart tells us what finally confirmed him in his endeavours. What we have here is a remarkable description of the process by means of which we are supposed to arrive at the negative judgement. The attentive reader will be able to see the whole series of errors in succession, and he will find that the negative judgement is actually presupposed long before the point at which it is finally supposed to emerge.

Sigwart proceeds from the correct observation that our first judgements are all positive. These judgements are evident and made with complete confidence. "But now", he says, "our thought goes out beyond the given; as a result of recollections and associations, other judgements are formed, also with the thought that they express what is real." (This means that the ideas are connected with a consciousness of objective validity, this being of the essence of judgement, according to Sigwart; sect. 14, p. 98.) These other judgements, he continues, might be exemplified by our "expecting to find some familiar thing in its usual place, or our assumption that we will be able to smell a certain flower. But now some part of what we thus suppose comes into *conflict* with what it is that we immediately know". (Sigwart does not attempt to show how we are able to recognize that something "conflicts" with what we know, if we are not yet able to make negative judgements and are not in possession of negative concepts. The difficulty becomes even more apparent as he continues.) "In such cases, when we do *not find* what we had expected, we become aware of the *difference* between what is *merely* thought about and what is real." (What does "not find" mean here? The phrase is one which, prior to this point, is not to be found. Clearly what I find, in the cases in question, is that something which I had expected to be accompanied by something else is in fact *without* that something else; but this is possible only to the extent that I am able to affirm the one and deny the other—i.e., affirm that the other does *not* accompany the one. And how are we to interpret the term "difference"? To be aware of a difference is to be aware, with respect to two things, that one of them is *not* the other. And, finally, what is the meaning of the phrase *"merely* thought about"? Clearly: something which is thought about but which is *not* at the same time real. Sigwart does not seem to realize that he has already allowed the negative judgement to come into play). He continues: "What we are immediately certain of is something *other* than that which we had expected." (Something other—i.e., something which is *not* the same, something which cannot possibly be the same.) "And now" (because of the fact that we have already made so many negative judgements) "negation finally enters into the picture, cancelling out the assumption in question and rejecting it as invalid. With this we have something *entirely new*; the subjective combination is separated from the consciousness of certainty. This subjective combination is contrasted with one that is certain and we recognize the difference between them; out of this the concept of invalidity arises." The final sentence would seem to result from sheer carelessness of expression. If the word "invalid" is to mean *false*, and not merely *uncertain*, then the concept of invalidity cannot be acquired by comparing a combination of ideas which is uncertain; what we need is a contrast between a combination which has been accepted and one which has been rejected. But actually the conflicting affirmative judgement is not at all required. The conflict—the incompatibility of certain characteristics—is already apparent from the relation between the concepts of the conflicting characteristics. Even Sigwart himself, if I may be permitted to repeat it, is aware that his conflict cannot be grasped by any attempt at a positive judgement (see p. 89n. and pp. 98ff.). It may well be that we often make negative judgements as a result of having first made the opposing positive judgement, but this is by no means the way in which *every* negative judgement comes about. Suppose, for example, I am asked: "Is there a regular figure with a thousand angles and a thousand and one sides?" It will have occurred to me previously, as may be the case with most people, that I cannot be at all sure that there is such a thing as a regular figure with a thousand angles. Hence I may make the negative judgement, on the basis of a conflict of characteristics, that there is no such figure—*without* having previously made an attempt at a positive judgement. It is not at all necessary, as Sigwart thinks it is, that I must first make a "confident assumption" that there is a regular figure with a thousand angles and a thousand and one sides.

The application of negation or denial is by no means restricted in the way in which Sigwart says it is. Sigwart betrays the fact that he realizes this too (see, e.g., p. 152 and even p. 150), despite his insistence that there can be no negative copula which performs a function of judgement on the same footing as affirmation or acceptance. It is false that, whenever a thing is denied, what it is that is denied is always the property "valid". Even in the case of a judgement, we can deny not only its validity, but also, among other things, its certainty, or its being *a priori*. The subject of the judgement may be treated in a similar way. One can deny certainty or validity of a judgement; one can deny modesty of a request; and, more generally, one can deny, of any *A*, a *B*. Sigwart himself makes such denials, just as everyone else does. Indeed, he often speaks with far more correctness than his theory would allow, thus instinctively bearing witness to the truth. According to his theory, the only thing that can be denied is validity, and this can only be denied of judgement; but he tells us, on p. 151 for example, that "of any subject, an *unlimited number of predicates* may be denied". This is certainly correct, and it is precisely for this reason that we are justified in retaining the ancient doctrine that there are two co-ordinate species of judgement.

## On the Concepts of Truth and Existence
### (Note 25 to page 18)

We use the expressions "true" and "false" in a number of quite different ways. Taking them in their strict and proper sense, we speak of true and false *judgements*; then (modifying the meanings somewhat) we also speak of true and false *things*, as when we speak of "a true friend" or "false gold." It is hardly necessary to observe that when I spoke in the lecture of *things* being true or false, I was using the terms in their derivative sense and not in their strict and proper sense. In this derivative use, we may say that the true is that which is, and the false that which is not. Just as Aristotle spoke of "ὂν ὡς ἀληθές," i.e., a being in the sense of the true, we might thus speak of a "ἀληθὲς ὡς ὄν," i.e., a true in the sense of a being.

It is often said that truth, in its strict sense, consists in a correspondence between a judgement and its object (in an *adequatio rei et intellectus*, as the scholastics had put it). This dictum is right in a certain sense, but it is easily misunderstood and has in fact led to serious errors. Some have taken the correspondence to be a kind of *identity* which holds between something in the judgement, or in the thought or idea at the base of the judgement, and something to be found outside the mind. But this cannot be the meaning of "to correspond" in the present context. It means rather "to be appropriate," "to be in harmony with", "to suit", "to be fitting to".

One could propose a similar view about the correctness of the emotions. In other words, one could say that the correctness of emotion also consists in a kind of correspondence between the emotion and its object. And this would also be right, if it were not misinterpreted. One loves or hates correctly provided that one's feelings are adequate to their object—adequate in the sense of being appropriate, suitable, or fitting. But it would be manifestly absurd to say that the correctness of love and hate consists in a kind of *identity* that holds between these feelings, or in the thought or idea on which they are based, and something lying outside the feelings; and it would be equally absurd to say that when such feelings are incorrect it is because of the absence of such identity. This misconception of the notion of adequacy or correspondence, along with a number of other errors, has brought the theory of judgement to the present unhappy state from which psychologists and logicians are trying so hard to free it.

The concepts of *existence* and *non-existence*, respectively, are correlates of the concepts of the truth of the (unitary) affirmative judgement and the truth of the (unitary) negative judgement. Judgement is correlated with what is judged, the affirmative judgement with what is judged affirmatively, the negative judgement with what is judged negatively; so, too, the correctness of the affirmative judgement is correlated with the *existence* of what is judged, and the correctness of the negative judgement is correlated with the *non-existence* of what is judged. To say that an affirmative judgement is true is to say no more nor less than that its object is existent; to say that a negative judgement is true is to say no more nor less than that its object is non-existent. It is one and the same logical principle that tells us, in the one case, that either the simple affirmative judgement or the simple negative judgement is true, and in the other case, that the object of the judgement is either existent or non-existent.

Thus, for example, the assertion of the truth of the judgement, "Some man is learned", is the correlate of the assertion of the existence of its object—namely, a learned man. And the correlate of the assertion of the truth of the judgement, "No stone is alive", is the assertion of the non-existence of its object—i.e., the non-existence of a living stone. Here, as elsewhere, correlative assertions are inseparable. The judgement "A is greater than B" and "B is smaller than A" are related in the same way, as are the judgements "A causes B" and "B is the effect of A".*

## On the Unity of the Concept of the Good
(Note 26 to page 18)

The concept of what is good in itself is thus univocal in the strict sense and not, as Aristotle taught, univocal only in an analogous sense. (Aristotle had been the victim of a confusion of which we shall speak later). German philosophers—for example, Kant, and more recently, Windelband—have also failed to grasp the unity of the concept. There is a defect in ordinary German that is likely to be misleading: We have no single expression to serve as the contrary of "*gut*". We must appeal to a variety of terms—for example, "*übel*" (evil), "*böse*" (wicked), "*arg*" (ill),

* [Editor's note: Brentano's later conception of truth is quite different. The thought that true judgements are correlated with "the existence of objects" and with "the non-existence of objects" is dropped altogether. He came to hold that the expressions "the existence of such-and-such" and "the non-existence of such-and-such" are only synsemantic and do not refer to anything at all. His later view is substantially this: an affirmative judgement is true provided its object is such that anyone who judged about it with evidence would accept or affirm it; and a negative judgement is true provided its object is such that anyone who judged about it with evidence would reject or deny it. For further details, see Brentano's *Wahrheit und Evidenz* (Hamburg: Felix Meiner, 1958), ed. Oskar Kraus; English translation, *The True and the Evident* (London: Routledge & Kegan Paul, 1966), ed., Roderick M. Chisholm. On the concept of a "unitary" [*einheitlich*] judgement, see Brentano's addendum to the second part of "Miklosich on Subjectless Propositions", below.]

"*schlimm*" (annoying), "*abscheulich*" (loathsome), "*schlecht*" (bad), and the like. And thus one is misled into thinking that, as is so often the case, the absence of a single term for the contrary of a concept indicates that the concept is not univocal. If there is no common concept for those things that are the opposite of what can be called "good", then one may wonder whether "good" is equivocal.

Of the various expressions I have mentioned, it seems to me that "*schlecht*" (bad), like the Latin "*malum*", is the one that is most generally applicable to designate the contrary of what is good (philologists whom I have consulted are of the same opinion), and I shall use it therefore as the contrary of "*gut*".

I have said that particular instances of the intentional relation of love and of hate all have something in common. This does not mean, however, that there are no *subspecies* of these relations. Thus even if "*schlecht*" (bad) is a truly general concept, applicable to anything that is the contrary of what is good, there may yet be subspecies within the general domain to which it applies, of which the one may suitably be called "*böse*" (wicked), another "*übel*" (evil), and so on.*

## On the Evident

(Note 27 to page 20)

The distinction between judgements which are evident and judgements which are blind is much too striking to have escaped notice altogether. Even the sceptical Hume is far from denying the distinction. According to what he says in the *Enquiry Concerning Human Understanding* (Section IV), the *evident* comprises analytic judgements (which are supposed to include the axioms and proofs of mathematics) and certain impressions; but these

---

* [Editor's note: According to Brentano's later view, such terms as "good" and "bad", like "true" and "false", are synsemantic and have no independent meaning. The point, expressed above, that "good" is a univocal term could be put, in accordance with the later view, by saying: the term "good" performs a uniform function in discourse; sentences in which "good" is ostensibly predicated of some thing all serve to indicate that any correct emotion that is directed upon the thing must be positive. See Brentano's *The True and the Evident*.]

latter do not include the so-called inferences from experience. Inferences from experience, according to Hume, are not the effects of reason, but the effects of a habit or custom which is entirely unreasonable; such beliefs are instinctive and mechanical. (See Section V.)

It is one thing, however, to take note of a fact, and another thing to provide a clear and distinct account of its nature. Given that the nature of judgement has been almost universally misconceived until very recent times, it is hardly to be expected that the nature of the evident would be properly understood. Even Descartes' usual discernment fails him here. He was very much concerned with the problem, however, as we may see from the following passage taken from the third of his Meditations: "When I say that I am so instructed by nature [he is referring to so-called external perception], I mean merely a certain *spontaneous inclination* which impels me to believe in this connection, and not a *natural light* which makes me recognize that it is true. But these two things are very different. For I cannot doubt that which the *natural light* causes me to believe to be true; as for example, it has shown me that I *am* from the fact that I doubt, or other facts of the same kind. And I possess no other faculty whereby to distinguish truth from falsehood, which can teach me that what this light shows me to be true is not really true, and no other faculty that is equally trustworthy. But as far as neutral impulses are concerned, I have frequently remarked, when I had to make active choice between virtue and vice, that they often led me to the part that was worse; and this is why I do not see any reason for following them in what regards truth and error."[1]

---

[1] Cum hic dico me ita doctum esse a natura intelligo tantum spontaneo quodam impetu me ferri ad hoc credendum, non lumine aliquo naturali mihi ostendi esse verum, quae duo multum discrepant. Nam quaecunque lumine naturali mihi ostenduntur (ut quod ex eo quod dubitem sequatur me esse, et similia) nullo modo dubia esse possunt, quia nulla alia facultas esse potest, cui aeque fidam ac lumini isti, quaeque illa non vera esse possit docere: sed quantum ad impetus naturales jam saepe olim judicavi me ab illis in deteriorem partem fuisse impulsum cum de bono eligendo ageretur, nec video cur iisdem in ulla alia re magis fidam. [English translation from the *Philosophical Works of Descartes*, trans. E. S. Haldane and G. R. T. Ross, Vol. I, pp. 160–1.]

We certainly cannot conclude from this passage that the concept of the evident escaped Descartes or that he failed to take note of the distinction between an insight (*Einsicht*) and a judgement which is blind. Yet, despite the fact that he took care to distinguish the class of judgements from that of ideas, he misplaces the distinguishing characteristic, evidence, which pertains always to the insightful judgement, and classifies it with ideas instead of with judgements. That form of perception which he called the *idea*—the presentation, that which is before the mind—is the basis of the judgement, and Descartes assumes that the idea is that which is evident. He even goes so far as to call this idea a "cognoscere"—an instance of knowing. A matter of knowing something and yet not a judgement! One might say that what we have here are vestigial organs in the development of psychology. After the great advances which Descartes himself made in the theory of judgement, they survive to remind us of a stage long since past. There is one point, however, with respect to which this phenomenon is to be distinguished from similar phenomena in the evolution of species. In the present case, the vestigial organs, not having adapted themselves to the stages that follow, become highly troublesome, with the result that Descartes' additional efforts on behalf of the theory of knowledge turn out to be in vain. To quote Leibniz, Descartes remains in the "antechamber of truth". It is only from this point of view that we are able to understand the peculiar hybrid character of Descartes' *clara et distincta perceptio*, of which it is so difficult to obtain a clear and distinct idea. If we are to find that which distinguishes insights from all other judgements, we must look for it in the inner peculiarities of the *act of insight* itself.

To be sure, there are those who have looked in the right place without having found what they were looking for. We have seen how Sigwart misconceives the nature of judgement. Judgement, according to him (*Logik*, sections 14 and 31, esp. 4 and 5), involves a relation between ideas and also a feeling of compulsion, or an irresistible impulse, which pertains to the ideas. This feeling, according to him, is to be found even in connection with the most blind of prejudices. In such cases it is not normative, but (Sigwart says explicitly) it is taken to be normative and universal. How do these cases differ, then, from insights? Sigwart says (in *op. cit.*, section 3, for example) that the evident character of a genuine insight is constituted by such a feeling. But the feeling which pertains to the insight is not merely one that is *taken* to be normative and universal; it must be one that *is* normative and universal.

The untenability of this theory seems to me to be obvious; there are many reasons for not accepting it.

(1) The peculiar nature of insight—the clarity and evidence of certain judgements which is inseparable from their truth—has little or nothing to do with a feeling of compulsion. It may well be that, at a given moment, I cannot help but judge in the way in which I do judge. But the clarity in question does not consist in any feeling of compulsion; no awareness of a compulsion to judge in a certain way could, as such, guarantee the truth of the judgement. One may reject indeterminism and thus hold that every judgement, given the circumstances under which it is made, is necessary; and yet one may deny, with perfect right, that every such judgement is true.

(2) In trying to locate the consciousness of an insight in the feeling of a compulsion to believe, Sigwart asserts that the consciousness of one's own compulsion is at the same time a consciousness of a similar necessity for every thinker to whom the same grounds are present. If he means that the one conviction is indubitably connected with the other, then he is mistaken. Given that on the basis of certain data one thinker is compelled to make a certain judgement, why should it be that every thinker on the basis of the same data would have a similar compulsion? One may be tempted, in this connection, to appeal to the general causal law according to which, if all the relevant conditions are the same, the effects will also be the same. But this general law is not applicable in the present case. For the relevant causal conditions will include all those psychical dispositions which may not enter directly into consciousness at all but which will exercise their effects upon one's judging; and these dispositions are different for different people. Misled by paralogisms, Hegel and his school have even denied the law of contradiction; and Trendelenburg, who opposes Hegel, has at least restricted its validity (Trendelenburg, *Abhandlungen über Herbarts Metaphysik*). Hence we can no longer say, as Aristotle did, that it is impossible for anyone inwardly to deny the principle—although for Aristotle himself,

to whom the principle was clearly evident, its denial was certainly impossible.

But it is true that anything that is seen to be evident by one person is certain, not only for him, but also for anyone else who sees it in a similar way. Moreover, any judgement which is thus seen by one person to be true is universally valid; its contradictory cannot be seen to be evident by any other person; and anyone who accepts its contradictory is *ipso facto* mistaken. What I am saying here pertains to the nature of truth: anyone who perceives something as true is also able to see that he is justified in regarding it as true for all. But it would be a gross confusion to suppose that this awareness of something being true for everyone implies an awareness of a universal compulsion to believe.*

(3) Sigwart entangles himself in a multiplicity of contradictions. He says—as he must if he is not to give in to scepticism or to abandon his entire logic—that judgements which are evident may be distinguished from judgements which are not, and that we can make the distinction in our own consciousness. Thus the one class of judgements, but not the other, must appear as normative and universal. But he also says that both classes of judgements—those which are evident and those which are not— are made with a consciousness of universal validity. The two types of judgement, therefore, would seem to present themselves in precisely the same way. If this were true, then one could make out the distinction between those of the first kind and those of the second only by further reflection—taking place either at the same time or later than the judgements—during the course of which one would appeal to some *criterion* or other as a kind of measuring rod. There are actually passages in which Sigwart says that there is an awareness of agreement with universal rules and that this awareness accompanies every perfectly evident judgement (cf., e.g., *op. cit.*, 2nd edn., section 39, p. 311). But this is hardly in agreement with our experience—it was possible to reason syllogistically with perfect evidence long before the discovery of the rules of the syllogism. And in any case, we must reject what Sigwart is saying here, for the rule to which he appeals is itself

* [Editor's note: This criticism, and this work in general, make clear that the refutation of so-called "psychologism" goes back to Brentano, and especially to the *Ursprung*.]

something that must be assured; such assurance would require either an infinite regress or a vicious circle.

(4) In his theory of self-consciousness, Sigwart becomes involved in still another contradiction (but one which, it seems to me, he could have avoided even after arriving at his erroneous conceptions of the nature of judgement and of evidence). What is expressed by "I exist" is said to be *merely* evident and to be quite unaccompanied by any feeling of compulsion or of universal necessity. (At any rate, this is the only way I am able to interpret the following passage from his *Logik*, 2nd edn., Vol. I, p. 310: "The certainty that I exist and that I think is basic and fundamental, the condition of all thought and of all certainty. Here one can speak only of direct evidence; one cannot even say that the thought is necessary, for it is prior to all necessity. Equally direct and evident is the conscious certainty that I think this or that; it is inextricably interwoven with my self-conscious in such a way that the one is give with the other.") Given the doctrines previously considered, this would seem to be a *contradictio in adjecto* and thus incapable of defence.

(5) Still more contradictions are to be found in Sigwart's peculiar and dubious theory of "postulates", which he contrasts with axioms. The certainty of axioms is said to lie in the compulsion we have to think in a certain way. But the certainty of postulates, according to Sigwart, is based upon our practical needs and not upon any purely intellectual motive (*op. cit.*, pp. 412ff.). Thus the law of causality, in his view, is a mere postulate and not an axiom; we take it to be certain because we find that, if we were not to accept it, we would be unable to investigate nature. But consider now the consequences, for Sigwart, of his accepting the law of causality in this way: out of sheer good will, he decrees that like conditions produce like effects; thus he is taking something to be true without any consciousness of being compelled to do so. But to say this is to contradict Sigwart's theory of judgement— unless, of course, taking something to be true is not the same as making a judgement. So far as I can see, Sigwart has only one way out: he ought to say that he does *not* believe any of the postulates, such as that of causation in nature, which he assumes to be "certain". But in such a case, he could no longer be serious.*

* [Editor's note: Brentano's conception of the universal validity of causation is set forth in detail in his *Vom Dasein Gottes* (Leipzig:

(6) The doctrine of postulates becomes even more question-able if we consider it along with what we have discussed under (2) above. The consciousness of a universal necessity to think in a certain way, according to Sigwart, is an axiom and not a postu-late. But this universal necessity to think in a given way is obvious to us only if we apply the law of causality to our own compulsion to think in that way. And then the law of causality itself is said to be a mere postulate and hence to be without evidence. The mark of axioms, according to Sigwart, is that they involve a universal compulsion or necessity to believe; hence it is only a postulate that there are such axioms. And therefore what Sigwart calls axioms are deprived of what they must have, according to him, if they are to be distinguished from his postulates. All this accords with Sigwart's remark (*op. cit.*, section 3) that the belief in the reliability of evidence is a "postulate". But given his interpretation of "postulate", I cannot imagine how such a remark is to fit in with the rest of the theory.

(7) Sigwart denies that there is any distinction between assertoric and apodictic judgements (*Logik*, section 31) for, he says, every judgement involves the feeling of necessity. This assertion must also be attributed to his erroneous conception of judgement; he would seem to identify the feeling, which he some-times calls the feeling of evidence, with the nature of apodicity. But this is to overlook the *modal* characteristic which distinguishes some evident judgements from the evident judgements of self-awareness; the law of contradiction would be an instance of the former, the judgement that I exist an instance of the latter. The former exemplifies what is "necessarily true or necessarily false", the latter what is only "actually true or false". Both are evident, however, and in the same sense of the word, and they do not differ with respect to certainty. It is only from judgements of the former sort, not from those of the latter sort, that we acquire the concepts of impossibility and necessity.*

Despite his polemic against conceiving apodictic judgements as a special class of judgement, Sigwart occasionally bears witness to the contrary view, as is clear from what was discussed under

* [Editor's note: See Appendix I.]

Felix Meiner, 1929), ed. Alfred Kastil, and his *Versuch über die Erkennt-nis* (Leipzig: Felix Meiner, 1925), ed. Alfred Kastil.]

(4) above. The knowledge expressed by "I exist", according to him (*op. cit.*, p. 312), is to be contrasted with our knowledge of axioms in that it pertains to a simple factual truth. Here he speaks more soundly than his general theory would allow.

Sigwart's theory of the evident, then, is essentially wrong. Like Descartes, he certainly took note of the phenomenon; and it must be said to his credit that he exercised great zeal in trying to analyze it. But like many others who have been concerned with the analysis of psychological phenomena, he seems not to have stopped at the right place in his eagerness to complete the analysis; the result was that he attempted to reduce one set of phenomena to another set of entirely different phenomena.

Obviously any mistake about the nature of the evident must be full of dire consequences for the logician. We could say that Sigwart's theory of the evident is the basic defect of his logic— were it not for his misconception of the nature of judgement in general. Again and again we find the unhappy results of his theory; an example is his inability to understand the general causes of error. The principal cause, he says in his *Logik* (Vol. I, 2nd edn., p. 103n), is the imperfection of our language; and this, surely, is a one-sided account.

Many other prominent logicians, of recent years, have fared no better than Sigwart with the theory of the evident. The views of the excellent John Stuart Mill—to cite only one example —are discussed in Note 68.

The fact that the nature of the evident is almost universally misunderstood explains why it is that we often hear the expression "more or less evident". Even Descartes and Pascal spoke in this way; but the expression is completely inappropriate. What is evident is certain; and certainty in the strict sense of the term knows no distinctions of degree. In a recent issue of the *Vierteljahrsschrift für wissenschaftliche Philosophie*, we are even told, in all seriousness, that there are *evident presumptions* which, despite their evidence, may well be *false*. Needless to say, I regard this as nonsense. I regret that my own lectures, given at a time when I took degrees of conviction to be a matter of intensity of judgement, seem to have been the occasion for such confusions.*

* [Editor's note: Brentano is here referring to A. Meinong's "Zur erkenntnistheoretischen Würdigung des Gedächtnis", *Vierteljahrsschrift für wissenschaftliche Philosophie*, Tenth Year (1886), pp. 7–33.]

## Ethical Subjectivism
(Note 28 to page 21)

Compare Hume's *Enquiry concerning the Principles of Morals*, which has already been cited. Some philosophers who have attempted to base ethics upon the feelings have shown more insight than Hume. (For example, Beneke and Überweg, who follows him; see the account of Beneke's ethical views in Volume III of Überweg's *Grundriss der Geschichte der Philosophie*.) Herbart comes closer to the truth when he speaks of "evident judgements of taste" and when he contrasts the beautiful with what is merely pleasing, ascribing universal validity and indubitable worth only to the former. (Strictly speaking, however, one should not use the expression "evident judgements of taste". For what we have here are really *feelings* and not *judgements* at all. And feelings, as such, are not evident but only analogous to what is evident.) Unfortunately, Herbart's views are mistaken in other respects, and he soon strays from the proper path, with the result that his practical philosophy is much farther from the truth than that of Hume.

Those who overlook the distinction between pleasure that is experienced as being correct and pleasure that is not so experienced are likely to fall into one or the other of two opposing errors. Thus some speak as though *all* pleasure is experienced as being correct, and others as though *no* pleasure is experienced as being correct. Those who take the latter course abandon altogether the concept of the good as being that which rightly pleases; "worthy of being desired" as distinguished from "capable of being desired" is said to be an expression without sense. But for those who take the former course, the expression "worthy of being desired" does at least remain an independent concept. When they say, "Whatever is capable of being desired for its own sake is something that is worthy of being desired for its own sake, something that is good in itself", they believe that they are not expressing a tautology. And obviously this is something they should say if they are to be consistent, and in fact many did say it. In the middle ages, for example, it was even taught by the great Thomas Aquinas, to whom Ihering has paid fresh tribute. (See for example, the *Summa Theologica*, I, Q. 80 and 82, Art. 2, ad 1, and elsewhere.)

But this doctrine cannot be made to fit the facts unless the concepts of good and bad are given an incorrect subjective interpretation, similar to the Protagorean interpretation of the concepts of truth and falsehood. According to such subjectivism within the sphere of judgement, each man is the measure of all things; hence it often happens that what is true for one man is false for another. Analogously, those who hold that only the good can be loved and only the bad can be hated must assume that, within the sphere of the emotions, each man is the measure of all things, of things that are good in themselves, that they are good, and of things that are bad in themselves that they are bad. If this assumption is correct, then it will often happen that one and the same thing is both good and bad in itself; it will be good in itself for those who love it for its own sake, and it will be bad in itself for those who hate it for its own sake. But this is absurd. The subjective falsification of the concept of the good is just as untenable as is the subjective falsification of the concepts of truth and existence which Protagoras defended. But it is much easier to slip into the subjectivistic error in the former case, where we are concerned with what is rightly pleasing or displeasing. The error infects most ethical systems today. Some embrace it openly, as Sigwart has recently done (see the *Vorfragen der Ethik*, p. 6); others fall into it without being clearly conscious of the subjectivistic nature of their views.[1]

[1] Some thinkers teach that each person's knowledge, pleasure, and perfection are the things that are good for him: their opposites are bad for him, and everything else indifferent in itself. Possibly they will object to my counting them among the subjectivists, since it may seem upon superficial consideration that they are advocating a theory of the good that is equally valid for all. But a more careful examination will show that according to this view there is *nothing* that is universally good. Thus my own knowledge would be said to be worthy of *my* love, but it would be said to be intrinsically indifferent for everyone else; and the knowledge that any other person has would be intrinsically indifferent for me. It is especially strange to find that theists often advocate a subjectivistic view of loving and willing in the case of mortals, while assuming that God, and God alone, applies an objective standard and is thus able to estimate each perfection without regard to person. And then they suppose that by setting up God as an objective and eternal judge, they can make their egoistic principles harmless in practice.

As I have said, once one accepts the view that nothing can please except to the extent that it is really good in itself, and nothing can displease except to the extent that it is really bad in itself, one has taken a path which, if followed consistently, can lead only to subjectivism.

In the celebrated controversy between Bossuet and Fenélon, the great Bishop of Meaux advocated what might be called a version of subjectivism. Though Fenélon's moral precepts were neither base nor unchristian, his theses were finally condemned by Rome, but without being declared to be heretical. Indeed, if his teachings were heretical, then so, too, would be the thought underlying those beautiful and inspired lines, sometimes attributed to St. Theresa, which have not only escaped ecclesiastical censure, but have also found their way into many Catholic prayer books, in an inadequate Latin translation. I translate them here directly from the Spanish:

Nicht Hoffnung auf des Himmels sel'ge Freuden
Hat Dir, mein Gott, zum Dienste mich verbunden,
Nicht Furcht, die ich vor ew'gem Graus empfunden,
Hat mich bewegt, der Sünder Pfad zu meiden.

Du, Herr, bewegst mich, mich bewegt Dein Leiden,
Dein Anblick in den letzten, bangen Stunden,
Der Geisseln Wut, Dein Haupt von Dorn umwunden,
Dein schweres Kreuz und—ach!—Dein bittres Scheiden.

Herr, Du bewegest mich mit solchem Triebe,
Dass ich Dich liebte, wär' kein Himmel offen,
Dich fürchtete, wenn auch kein Abgrund schreckte;
Nichts kannst Du geben, was mir Liebe weckte;
Denn würd' ich auch nicht, wie ich hoffe, hoffen,
Ich würde dennoch lieben, wie ich liebe.

[This poem may be paraphrased as follows:

It is not hopes of heavenly bliss
That have bound me to your service, O God;
It was not fear of eternal torment
That persuaded me to avoid the path of the sinner.

It was you and your sufferings that moved me, Lord:
Your visage in the last fearful hours.
The fury of the scourge, the crown of thorns on your brow,
Your heavy cross—and your bitter farewell.

This becomes evident once one concedes (as at first one may not) that one and the same phenomenon may give rise to contrary tastes—to pleasure in one case and to displeasure in another. One may be tempted to argue that in such cases, although the external stimuli are the same, the corresponding subjective ideas or presentations must be essentially different. But this is impossible in the cases where we repeatedly experience one and the same phenomenon and then, as a result of an increase in age or a change in our habits, come to feel quite differently about it, experiencing it now with displeasure instead of with pleasure,

> Lord, you move me so strongly
> That I would love you if there were no entrance to heaven
> And would fear you if there were no threat of hell.
> You cannot give me anything to make me love you:
> If you had nothing to give, I would not hope as I do,
> But I would love you just as I do now.]

The views of Thomas Aquinas have often been presented as though they were pure subjectivism. It is true that much of what he says has a subjectivistic tone. (See for example, *Summa Theologica*, I, Q. 80, Art. 1, and note in particular the objections and replies, as well as the passages in which he states that one's own happiness is the highest final end for each person. He even says that each of the saints in heaven rightly desires his own blessedness more than that of all others.) But there are also statements showing that he rises above this subjectivistic viewpoint. For example, he says (as Plato and Aristotle had said before him, and as Descartes and Leibniz were to say afterwards) that everything that exists is as such something that is good, and good not merely as a means but also in itself. This last is a point the pure subjectivist explicitly denies (as Sigwart has recently done in his *Vorfragen der Ethik*, p. 6). Aquinas also says that if—what is in fact impossible—one had to choose between one's own eternal damnation and an injury to the divine love, then it would be right to prefer one's own eternal unhappiness.

In this latter instance, the moral feelings of Western Christianity are the same as those of the heathen Hindu, expressed in the rather strange story of the maiden who renounced her own eternal blessedness for the salvation of the rest of the world. The positivistic philosopher, Mill, expresses the same sentiment when he writes that, rather than bow in prayer before a being who is not truly good, "to hell I will go". I knew a Catholic priest who voted for Mill in a parliamentary election just because of this remark.

or conversely (see Section 25 of the lecture). There is no doubt but that contrary feelings may be directed upon one and the same phenomenon. This is also confirmed where an idea or presentation is instinctively repellent to us and yet arouses at the same time a higher type of pleasure (see Note 32 of the lecture).

If it were reasonable to suppose that every positive feeling or emotion is correct and that no such feeling or emotion ever contradicts another, then it would also be reasonable to suppose that the same is true of acts of preference. But this latter is so obviously false that those who hold the former view explicitly deny it and insist that, so far as contrary preferences are concerned, one is correct and the other incorrect.

Looking away from the medieval Aristotelians and going back to the master himself, we find that his own doctrine was quite different. He was aware of the distinction between correct and incorrect desires (ὄρεξις ὀρθὴ καὶ οὐκ ὀρθή) and knew that what is desired (ὀρεκτόν) is not always what is good (ἀγαθόν) (*De Anima*, Book III, Chapter 10). In the *Nicomachaean Ethics* (Book X, Chapter 3), he says that not every pleasure (ἡδονή) is good; there is such a thing as taking pleasure in the bad, and this is itself bad. In the *Metaphysics* (Book XII, Chapter 7, 1072a 28), he distinguishes between a lower and a higher type of desire (ἐπιθυμία and βούλησις); what is desired for its own sake by the higher type of desire is truly good. Here we are very close to the correct conception. It is especially interesting to find (as I did after presenting the lecture) that Aristotle had observed the analogy between ethical subjectivism and the logical subjectivism of Protagoras and that he repudiates both (*Metaphysics*, Book XI, Chapter 6, 1062b 12 and 1063a 10). But in the lines that immediately follow this passage, he seems to say, incorrectly, that we can recognize the good as good without any excitation of the emotions (compare *De Anima*, Book III, Chapters 9 and 10).

The temptation leading to such an error is easy to understand. It undoubtedly explains why Aristotle denies in the *Nichomachaean Ethics* (Book I, Chapter 6) that there is a univocal concept of the good (meaning thereby the concept of what is good in itself) and why he says that the goodness of rational thinking, of seeing, of joy, are united only by analogy. And it also explains why he says in the *Metaphysics* (Book VI, Chapter 4, 1027b 25) that the true and the false, unlike the good and the bad, are not in things. The former predicates, he says, are ascribed to things only in relation to certain psychological acts—namely, true and false judgements—as when we say "a true God" or "a false friend". But the predicates good and bad, he continues, are not thus ascribed to things merely in relation to a particular class of psychological activities. This is all incorrect, but it is an inevitable consequence of the error we have noted. Aristotle is closer to the correct view of the source of our concept and knowledge of the good when, in the *Nichomachaean Ethics* (Book X, Chapter 3), he argues against the doctrine that pleasure cannot be good. His argument is that everyone desires it. He adds: "If only irrational beings desired it, there might be something in what is said. But if rational creatures do so as well, what sense can there be in this view?" And this assertion can also be reconciled with the erroneous part of Aristotle's theory. In this respect, then, the moralists of sentiment, such as Hume, have an advantage over Aristotle, for they may correctly ask: How is one to know that a thing is worthy of being loved if one does not have the experience of love?

I have said that the temptation into which Aristotle fell seems quite understandable. It may be traced to the fact that whenever we have a positive emotion that is experienced as being correct, we also acquire the knowledge that the object of the emotion is something that is good. It is easy to confuse the relation between the emotion and the knowledge. One may then assume, mistakenly, that the love of the good thing is a consequence of the knowledge that it is good, and that the love is seen to be correct because it is seen to be appropriate to the knowledge.

It is interesting to compare this error of Aristotle concerning the experience of correct emotion with the analogous error that Descartes had made in the case of judgement (see Note 27, "On the Evident"). In each case, the philosopher in question tries to find the distinguishing mark in some peculiarity of the *idea* or presentation that lies at the basis of the psychological act, instead of looking, as he should have, toward the *act* itself which is experienced as being correct. Indeed, it seems clear to me from various passages in Descartes' book, "*Les Passions*", that he viewed correct emotion in substantially the same way that Aristotle did and that he held an analogous theory of the evident.

At the present time, there are many who come close to making the error that Descartes had made with respect to the nature of the evident (or perhaps we should say, they *do* make this error, implicitly). They seem to hold that every evident judgement can be seen to be evident upon the basis of some criterion, which would have to be given in advance. Either the criterion itself would have to be *known*, in which case there would be an infinite regress, or—and this is the only alternative—it would have to be given in the idea or presentation that underlies the judgement. As in the previous case, the temptation to make this error is easy to understand, and doubtless it had its effect upon Descartes. Aristotle's error is less common, though probably only because the phenomenon of an emotion being experienced as correct has received less attention than the evident judgement. Many have misconceived the latter, but few have even given the former enough consideration to be able to misconceive it.

## Two Unique Cases of Preferability
(Note 37 to page 29)

If our account of preferability is to be exact and exhaustive, we should consider two further important cases that were not mentioned in the lecture. The one case may be described as feeling pleasure in the bad, and the other as feeling displeasure in the bad.

What of pleasure in the bad? Is it itself something that is good? Aristotle says that it is not, and in a certain sense he is undoubtedly right. He writes in the *Nichomachaean Ethics* (Book X, Chapter 3, 1174a, 1-4): "No one would wish to feel joy in what is base, even if he were assured that no harm would come from it". The hedonists expressed the contrary view, and they include even such high-minded men as Fechner (see his work on the highest good). But their view is to be rejected. As Hume remarked, their practice is happily much better than their theory. Yet there is a grain of truth in what they say.

Pleasure in the bad is, as pleasure, something that is good, but at the same time, as an incorrect emotion, it is something that is bad. Even if it is predominantly bad, because of this incorrectness, it cannot be said to be purely bad. If, therefore, we reject it as bad, we are performing an act of preference in which freedom from what is bad is given preference over something else that is good. If we are able to see that it is correct to reject such pleasure as being bad, it must be because the act of preference is experienced as being correct.

What of displeasure in the bad? If displeasure in the bad is experienced as being correct, is it itself something that is good? Consider what occurs when a magnanimous person is pained at the sight of innocent victims of injustice, or when a man feels remorse about some misdeed that he has committed in the past. Now we have the reverse of the situation previously considered. Here we have a feeling that strikes us as being predominantly but not purely good. Its goodness is not like that of the exalted joy we would feel if the object of our emotion were the contrary of what it is that pains us or makes us feel regret. And this offers a justification for Descartes' advice that we ought rather to direct our attention and emotions upon the good. All this we recognize easily. Thus we have yet another case in which a preference that is experienced as being correct enables us to know what things are preferable to others.

In order not to introduce too many complications, I did not discuss these cases in the lecture. I felt that the omission was justifiable, since for all practical purposes the same results could be obtained if the hate that is experienced in these cases as being correct were treated simply as an instance of disliking or aversion (this is what Aristotle had done in the case of shameful joy), and if the love that is experienced as being correct were treated simply as an instance of liking or attraction.

Here, then, we have two rather special cases pertaining to the possible quantitative relations between the goodness and badness of pleasure and displeasure, on the one hand, and the correctness and incorrectness of emotion, on the other (compare also what is said in Note 31). These make clear that there is little hope of finding a generally valid way of filling in the great gaps in our ethical knowledge that were referred to in the lecture.*

* [Editor's note: These points are refined in Brentano's *Untersuchungen zur Sinnespsychologie* (Leipzig: Duncker & Humblot, 1907). Brentano there distinguishes between nonsensuous emotions (simple evaluations and preferences) and the sensuous side-effects (*Redundanzen*) which they cause (the sensations of pleasure and pain which may vary in their intensities). These blend into a single consciousness, but the different elements can be separated by conceptual analysis. The

SUPPLEMENTARY NOTES

## On the Charge of Excessive Rigorism
(Note 42 to page 32)

In his *Vorfragen der Ethik* (p. 42), Sigwart insists that one must not demand more of the human will than it is capable of performing. This doctrine, which is most surprising coming from the lips of so decided an indeterminist (compare his *Logik*, Vol. II, p. 592), hangs together with his subjectivistic conception of the good—a combination that can hardly be satisfactory to anyone who takes these questions seriously. (Note the way in which Sigwart himself, on page 15, slides over from egoism to a concern for the general good.)

But others have expressed similar opinions. One might really begin to wonder whether the sublime command to order all our actions by reference to the highest practical good is the correct ethical principle. For, aside from cases of insufficient reflection, which are not here to the point, the demand that we surrender ourselves completely to the highest good may well seem too severe. There is no one—no matter how upright his conduct may be—who can honestly look into his heart and deny these words of Horace:

> Nunc in Aristippi furtim praecepta relabor,
> Et mihi res, non me rebus subiungere conor.

But the doubt is unfounded. A comparison may make things clear. It is certain that no man can entirely avoid error. Nevertheless, avoidable or not, every erroneous judgement is a judgement that ought not to have been made, a judgement in conflict with the requirements of logic, and these cannot be modified. The rules of logic are not to be given up merely because of the weakness of our powers of reasoning. Similarly, the rules of ethics are not to be given up because of weakness of will. If a man is weak willed, ethics cannot cease to demand from him

---

purely sensuous constituents are to be evaluated separately from the nonsensuous constituents that cause them. In the case of remorse, for example, the nonsensuous emotion of regret is something that is in itself correct; but the sensuous "pangs of regret" to which the remorse gives rise are sensations which are not in themselves correct—they are useful, but in and for themselves they are an evil. See sections 25 and 26 of "Loving and Hating", Appendix IX of the present book.]

that he love what is known to be good, prefer what is known to be better, and place the highest good above all else. Even if one could show (and one cannot) that there are circumstances under which no one could remain true to the highest good, there would not be the slightest justification for setting aside the requirements of ethics. The one and only correct rule would remain evident and unalterably true: Give preference in every case to that which is better.

J. S. Mill feared that this demand would lead to endless self-reproach which would embitter the life of every individual. But such self-reproach is not itself one of the requirements of ethics; indeed the rule excludes it. Goethe was aware of this. These lines of his were not intended to encourage laxity:

> Nichts taugt Ungeduld,
> Noch weniger Reue,
> Jene vermehrt die Schuld,
> Diese schafft neue.

> [Impatience does us no good;
> Even less does rue.
> The first increases the old fault;
> The second creates a new.]

He refers here to impatience with one's own limitations; one should not submit to pangs of conscience when only a fresh and cheerful resolution will avail.

The same sentiment is expressed in the following lines, which I once found in an album, written in the hand of the pious Abbott Haneberg, who later became Bishop of Spires:

> Sonne dich mit Lust an Gottes Huld,
> Hab' mit allen,—auch mit dir Geduld!

> [Bask with pleasure in the grace of God;
> Have patience with everyone—including yourself.]

## Criticism of Ihering
(Note 45 to page 34)

Philosophers and jurists alike have emphasized that the law imposes restrictions in order to protect those spheres which should be at the disposal of the individual will. See, for example, Herbart's

*Idee des Rechts.* Ihering confirms this with numerous citations in his *Geist des römischen Rechts* (Book III, Chapter 1, p. 320n.). Arndt, in his *Handbuch der Pandekten,* defines law as "the supremacy of the will with respect to an object"; Sintenis defines law as "the will of one person elevated to the general will"; Windschneid defines it as "the content of a certain volition which the legal code declares shall be given expression in a given case in preference to any other". And Puchta, who may have expressed the thought in the greatest variety of ways, writes in his *Pandekten* (Section 22): "Men are called persons to the extent that they are potentially subject to such a will. . . . Personality is therefore the subjective possibility of a legal will, of a legal power." When speaking in the same work (Section 118, Note b) of the absence of personality, he observes that "the principle of modern law is the ability to dispose of one's own powers". He makes the same point in many other ways.

These legal authorities have concentrated their attention exclusively upon legal duties, not touching upon the ethical question as to how the individual will should manage its affairs within its own legitimate sphere. But Ihering has taken them to mean that the highest good, and the true end at which the legal code aims, is the pleasure that the individual takes in the activities of his own will. And so he writes: "The final goal of all law is, for them, willing" (*op. cit.,* pp. 320, 325); "The end of law (according to them) consists ultimately in the power and supremacy of the will" (p. 326). Given this interpretation of what the legal authorities have said, it is easy to understand why Ihering rejects it and succeeds in making it appear ridiculous. "According to this view", he says (p. 320), "the whole domain of individual rights is nothing more than an arena in which the will moves and exercises itself. The will is supposed to be the faculty by means of which the individual enjoys the law. This enjoyment is thought to consist in the satisfaction and glory of power that the individual feels when he exercises his legal rights—for example, when he arranges a mortgage or brings legal action, thus documenting the fact that he is a legal personality. What a poor thing the will would be if its proper 'sphere of activity' were restricted to these pedestrian legal activities!"

The legal authorities in question do regard the *immediate* aim of law as the setting of limits to what is at the disposal of the in-

94

dividual will. Had they intended thereby to disavow all concern for the *ultimate ethical end*, namely, the promotion of the highest practical good, they would deserve to be ridiculed. But there is no ground at all for this charge. If there is anything ridiculous here, it would seem to be the zeal with which Ihering has conducted his attack upon an army of straw men.

And his own proposal is hardly a satisfactory substitute. According to him, the sphere that the law assigns to the individual is simply one in which the individual's egoism is given free reign (a view which, as author of the later *Zweck im Recht*, he may no longer hold). He thus proposes this definition: "Law is the legal security for enjoyment" (p. 338). It would have been much better had he said: "Law is the legal security for the undisturbed exercise of individual power in the advancement of the highest good." Are violations of law the only type of bad conduct? Not at all. Our legal duties have their limits, but duty in general has jurisdiction over *all* our actions. This is emphasized by our popular religion—when it says, for example, that the individual must render an account for every idle word.

Ihering's first objection, then, was based upon a simple misunderstanding of what was intended. He also made other objections, but these seem to have been occasioned merely by imperfections in the use of language. He points out that if law is essentially a matter of setting limits to the activity of the individual will, so that one person will not disturb another in his efforts to promote the good, then one could say, of those persons who have, or have had, or will have no will, that they also have no legal rights. I say "have, or have had, or will have", since we must consider the past and the future as well as the present. A man who is dead often exercises an influence extending into the distant future. As Comte well said: "The living are increasingly dominated by the dead". There are circumstances, similarly, under which we may leave a decision to the future, thus renouncing the domain of our will, so to speak, in favour of some future will. This fact alone is sufficient to resolve a number of the paradoxes urged by Ihering (see pp. 320–325), but it does not resolve them all. Concern for the highest practical good does not require that an incurable imbecile be assigned a domain for the exercise of his will, for he has no will to exercise. Strictly speaking, therefore, he cannot be said to have any legal rights, according to our conception. Yet he is said to have a right to his own life. And sometimes we refer to such a person as the owner of a great estate and even say that he has a right to the crown and to the powers that go along with it. But if we examine the situation carefully, we will see that a subject incapable of responsibility is not hereby assigned legal rights. The legal rights and duties pertain to certain *other* individuals. Thus there are the rights and duties of the father who in his will makes provisions with respect to his property which will provide for the imbecile child. And when the imbecile is considered to have a right to his life, the legal domain that is involved is actually that of the state itself. For, in addition to the fact that murder is a violation of our duty to love, the state permits no one else to take a human life, and thus it sometimes even imposes a punishment in the case of attempted suicide.

Ihering makes still a third objection, saying that if legal rights are determined by reference to the spheres of individual wills, then the most foolish dispositions of will must be given legal validity. But it is easy to deal with this objection in the light of what we have said. Certainly, the state will permit its citizens to exercise their wills in foolish and senseless ways. Otherwise the state alone would have the right of making final decisions and there would be no individual rights. Those who hold the power of government are also capable of making foolish and senseless decisions, and as long as this is so, the state should not have all the power in its hands. But all secondary moral principles admit of exceptions, and it is often necessary for the state to expropriate the property of private individuals. And at times the state may annul senseless arrangements, or arrangements that have lost all relevance to the highest practical good. Here, as in every other so-called collision of duties, concern for the highest practical good is what must be decisive.

## Mill's Conception of the Evident
### (Note 68 to page 43)

It is not surprising that Hume would be guilty of this confusion [between expectation that is instinctive and habitual, and expectation that is justified by the principles of the calculus of probability]. For at the time he wrote, psychology was far less developed than it is now and study of the probability calculus had not yet sufficiently clarified the process of rational induction. But it is surprising to find that James Mill and Herbert Spencer did not advance in the slightest beyond Hume (see James Mill's *Analysis of the Phenomena of the Human Mind*, Vol. I, Chapter 9 and note 108) and that even the excellent J. S. Mill never saw the essential distinction between the two procedures—this despite the fact that Laplace's *Essai Philosophique sur les Probabilités* was at his disposal. Mill's failure to recognize the purely analytic character of mathematics and the general significance of the deductive procedure is connected with the same point. He had even denied that the syllogism leads to new knowledge. If one bases mathematics upon induction, then, of course, one cannot justify induction mathematically, for this would lead to a vicious circle. So far as this point is concerned, Jevons' *Logic* is beyond question the more nearly adequate.

But there is reason to believe that Mill had some inkling of the distinction we have referred to. In a note to his edition of James Mill's *Analysis of the Phenomena of the Human Mind* (Volume I, Chapter 11, p. 407), he criticizes his father's theory in the following terms: ". . . if belief is only an inseparable association, belief is a matter of *habit* and accident, and not of *reason*. Assuredly an association, however close, is not a sufficient *ground* of belief\*; it is not *evidence* that the corresponding facts are united in external nature. The theory seems to annihilate all distinction between the belief of the wise, which is *regulated by evidence*, and conforms to the real successions and co-existences of the facts of the universe, and the belief of fools, which is *mechanically produced* by any accidental association that suggests the idea of a succession or co-existence to the mind; a belief aptly characterized by the popular expression, 'believing a thing because they have taken it into their heads". This is all excellent. But it is robbed of its essential worth when Mill writes in a subsequent note (*op. cit.*, p. 438, note 110): "It must be conceded to him [the author of the *Analysis*] that an association, sufficiently strong to exclude all ideas that would exclude itself, *produces a kind of mechanical belief*; and that the processes by which the belief is corrected, or reduced to rational

\* [The italics up to this point are Mill's; the remaining ones are Brentano's.]

grounds, *all consist in the growth of a counter-association* tending to raise the idea of a disappointment of the first expectation, and as the one or the other prevails in the particular case, the belief or expectation exists or does not exist exactly as if the belief were the the same thing with the association." There is much here to give one pause. Mill refers to ideas that mutually exclude one another. What sort of ideas could these be? Mill tells us elsewhere that he knows "no case of absolute incompatibility of thought . . . except between the presence of something and its absence" (*op. cit.*, Vol. I, pp. 98–9, note 30). But are even these thoughts incompatible? Mill himself tells us the opposite elsewhere. He says that along with the thought of being there is always given at the same time the thought of non-being: "We are only conscious of the presence [of objects] by comparison with their absence" (p. 26, note 39). But aside from all this, how strange it is that Mill here allows the distinctive nature of the evident to escape him entirely and retains only that blind and mechanical formation of judgement which he had rightly looked down upon! So far as this point is concerned, the sceptic Hume stands far higher than Mill. For Hume sees at least that no such empirical conception of induction can satisfy the requirements of reason. Sigwart's criticism of Mill's theory of induction (*Logik*, Vol. II, p. 371) is basically sound. But in turning to his own "postulates", he does not provide us with any satisfactory alternative.

## *Miklosich on Subjectless Propositions**

### I

"*Subjektlose Sätze*" is the title which the distinguished linguist has now given this little work which was originally entitled, "*Die Verba Impersonalia im Slavischen*".

The change of title may well be connected with the significant additions to be found in the second edition, but actually it would have been more suitable for the first edition, too. For the author is not concerned with the nature of just *one* group of languages;

* [Discussion of Franz Miklosich, *Subjektlose Sätz* (Vienna: Braumüller, 1883); reprinted from the *Wiener Zeitung*, November 13 and 14, 1883, and included as an appendix to the first edition of *Vom Ursprung sittlicher Erkenntnis*.]

he is concerned with a thesis that is of much more extensive significance. If it is in conflict with the prevailing view, it is all the more worthy of investigation. The question is of interest, not only for philology, but also for psychology and metaphysics. What the author has to say should be welcomed, not only by those who are investigating these learned areas, but also by the schoolboy who is now tormented by his schoolmaster with impossible and incomprehensible theories (see Miklosich, p. 23ff.).

But actually the treatise has not had the influence it deserves. The contrary views still hold sway. The reappearance of the monograph indicates that the work is of interest to certain wider circles, but this is not to be attributed to the fact that the work is thought to have thrown light upon previous doubts and errors. Thus Darwin's epoch-making work, quite apart from the question of whether or not its hypothesis was correct, had incontestable value even for those who rejected it. One could only admire the wealth of important observations and ingenious conjectures that it contained. So, too, in the case of Miklosich. He has compressed into a few pages a rich store of learning, interspersed with the most subtle perceptions. Those who reject his principle thesis may yet be greatly indebted to him for points of detail.

Let us first consider the central question with which the work is concerned, and indicate briefly its significance.

According to an ancient doctrine of logic, all judgement is a matter of relating ideas; some judgements were said to combine ideas and others to separate them. This doctrine, which has been accepted almost unanimously for the past few thousand years, has exercised considerable influence upon disciplines other than logic. Thus grammarians have long held that the categorical judgement, in which a subject is combined with a predicate, is the simplest form that a judgement can take.

When we ask ourselves whether this doctrine is really true, we find that it involves certain difficulties. These difficulties could not permanently be kept out of sight, but most investigators held to the doctrine so firmly that they felt no inclination to question its universal validity. Propositions such as "It is raining" and "It is lightening" look as though they had no wish to conform to the doctrine. It was necessary, therefore, to conduct a search—to find subjects for these propositions so that they, too, might be put into categorical form. And many thought that they had found the proper subjects. But then, in strange contrast to the unity that had prevailed up to that point, they headed off in a great variety of directions. If we examine the various hypotheses that were proposed, we can readily see why there was no general agreement and why none of them could really be permanently satisfactory.

Science explains by conceiving a multiplicity as a unity. Attempts were made to do the same thing here, but none of the attempts was satisfactory. Thus it was held that when we say, "It is raining", the unnamed subject designated by means of the indefinite "it" is in fact Zeus; the proposition tells us that Zeus rains. But in "It is noisy", it would seem obvious that Zeus cannot be the subject. And so others assumed that in this latter case the subject is actually noise; what the proposition tells us is that the noise is noisy. Applied to the previous example, this hypothesis would have it that raining, or the rain, is what rains.

When we say in German, "*Es fehlt an Geld*", the meaning would have to be "*Das Fehlen an Geld fehlt an Geld*" ["There lacks money" would tell us that the lack of money is what lacks money]. But this is absurd. So it was said that in this case "*Geld*" was the real subject; hence the proposition would tell us that money is what lacks money. But if this type of proposition requires special handling, then the desired unity of explanation is threatened. Perhaps by closing one eye we may partially conceal this fact from ourselves. But then what are we to do with "*Es gibt einen Gott*" ["There is a God", or, literally, "It gives a God"]? We can hardly render "It gives a God" as "The giving of a God gives a God", or "The giving gives a God", or "God gives a God".

And so the philologists had to look for an entirely different type of explanation. But where was it to be found? Perhaps, they thought, some new expedient could be found for dealing with the last example. But if we have to modify our hypothesis for each new case that comes along, we have produced only a caricature of a genuinely scientific explanation. No single hypothesis was advanced which could deal with all these cases—with the possible exception of a hint by Schleiermacher. If this learned man really said, as has been reported (Miklosich, page 16), that the subject of these propositions is *Chaos*, we have to assume, not that he was offering still another hypothesis, but only that he was ridiculing what the philologists had been able to do with their problem.

Some hold that the true subjects of such propositions as "It is raining" and "It is lightening" have not yet been discovered and think that science still faces the task of finding the subjects. But if these propositions really do have subjects which people think of but leave unexpressed when they assert them, why should they be so difficult to find? Steinthal tries to explain this by saying that the grammatical subject which is denoted by these propositions is a certain Something, which is not thinkable but is somehow alluded to. Many will prefer to say with Miklosich (p. 23): "We are not going too far when we say that grammar is not concerned with the unthinkable."

Miklosich says that the supposed subject in the case of these propositions is a delusion. The propositions do not involve combining a subject and a predicate; they are, as he puts it, subjectless. He bases his assertion on the totality of phenomena that are involved and upon the grotesque failures of the various attempts, often highly ingenious, to find subjects for these propositions.

There are other observations that will confirm his view. Among these is one consideration about the nature of judgement that is of special significance. Miklosich opposes those who, like Steinthal, think there is no real relationship between grammar and logic. He also defends his views against those who have attacked them on the basis of psychological and logical considerations. And he arrives at the conclusion that, because of the peculiar characteristics of one type of judgement, we should expect to find subjectless propositions in language. As he points out, it is not true that every judgement is a matter of relating one concept to another. A judgement is often merely the affirmation or denial of a simple fact. In such a case, the proper linguistic expression clearly cannot be one in which there is a combination of a subject and a predicate. Miklosich notes that there have been philosophers who were aware of this fact but, as he observes, they did not usually appreciate its significance. They were not entirely clear about the matter and, despite some indecision, they were disinclined to give up the traditional view and ended up by denying what it was that they first affirmed. Thus Trendelenburg concluded that "It is lightening", strictly speaking, does not express a judgement. It expresses only the rudiments of a judgement, he said; it makes way for the concept of lightning and serves to fix it, thus providing a ground for the complete judgement, "Lightning is conducted by iron". And Herbart concluded that judgements such as "It is noisy" are not judgements in the ordinary sense, nor are they, strictly speaking, what is meant in logic by judgement. There is an excellent passage (p. 21f.) in which Miklosich shows that these philosophers actually contradict themselves and traces their mistakes back to a misunderstanding of the nature of judgement and to an inadequate definition of it.

Miklosich concludes from all this that the existence of subjectless propositions is beyond doubt. And he shows that they are by no means as uncommon as the controversy about them might lead one to believe. There is a great variety of them, which he classifies in the second part of his treatise (pp. 33 to 72). Thus he lists subjectless propositions with a *Verbum activum*, subjectless propositions with a *Verbum reflexivum*, subjectless propositions with a *Verbum passivum*, and subjectless propositions with the *Verbum esse*, and he cites countless examples of each type from a great variety of languages. In connection with the first type in particular, he makes an eightfold division, grouping the propositions with respect to differences of content. He notes as a general principle (p. 6) that the *Verbum finitum* of subjectless propositions is always in the third person singular and, where differences in gender are utilized, it is always neuter.

He also considers the matter in many other connections. He shows that, historically, subjectless propositions did not come into being after subject-predicate propositions; they existed from the very first (p. 13ff., p. 19), but in the course of time they disappeared from some languages (p. 26). He notes that the languages in which they are preserved have an advantage, since the use of subjectless propositions can enliven the language (p. 26). And he cites still other reasons for denying that these propositions can be put into the subject-predicate form that is supposed to be equivalent to them. The German "*Mich friert*" [It makes me cold] cannot be identified with "*Ich friere*" [I am cold]; otherwise we would have to identify "*Was frierst du draussen? Komme doch herein!*" [What are you doing freezing out there? Come right in!]

with "*Was friert dich's draussen? Komme doch herein!*" [What is it that is making you freeze out there? Come right in!] "The expression '*Mich friert*' cannot be used if I expose myself voluntarily to the cold" (p. 37).

## II

This, in brief, is the content of the book. I shall now permit myself a few critical remarks.

It should be clear that I not only approve of this treatise in general, but also that I accept its basic theses. The proofs are put so cogently that even those who are putting up a struggle will be unable to resist the truth. Quite independently of these proofs, I arrived long ago at the same view of the basis of a purely psychological analysis, and I gave it unequivocal public expression when I published my *Psychologie* in 1874.

I took great pains to put the view in a clear light and to show that the previous theories were untenable. But up to now what I said does not seem to have had much effect. A few have agreed with me, but for the most part I have had no more success in convincing philosophers than Miklosich, in his first edition, had had in convincing philologists. We are confronted here with a prejudice that has been sending out roots for thousands of years; it has forced its way into our elementary schools, and it is now looked upon as a fundamental principle upon which a host of others depend. We should not expect, therefore, that the error will simply disappear once it has been refuted. It is more likely that the new point of view will be distrusted and that the grounds upon which it is based will not be properly evaluated. But now two investigators have arrived at this point of view, working entirely independently of each other and approaching the topic from quite different directions. Perhaps we have a right to hope that this fact will not be looked upon as a mere coincidence and that due attention will be given to the evidence, particularly to the new edition of Miklosich's treatise, in which I am happy to find my own work considered.

Since I am in agreement with respect to the principal theses of the treatise, my disagreement with respect to certain subordinate points is of no great significance. But I shall mention some of these.

Miklosich uses the expression "subjectless propositions" to

refer to those simple propositions in which there is no combination of subject and predicate. I agree entirely that there are such propositions, but I am not happy with the expression "subjectless proposition" in this context or with the reasons that Miklosich has given for using it.

Subject and predicate are correlative concepts and they stand and fall together. If a proposition is truly subjectless, then, by the same token, it is also truly predicateless. For this reason it does not seem to me to be appropriate to describe the propositions in question merely as "subjectless"; and it is quite incorrect to describe them, as Miklosich sometimes does (see pp. 3, 25, 26, and elsewhere), by saying they are merely "predicate propositions" [*Prädikatsätze*]. This manner of speaking might lead one to think that Miklosich, too, thinks that in these propositions there is a concept, namely the subject, which is understood and left unexpressed; but of course he explicitly denies this (p. 3f., and elsewhere). Or one might assume that he looked upon these propositions as a type of stunted subject-predicate proposition which were originally of the subject-predicate form; but he explicitly denies this, too (p. 13ff.). Actually, his view may be put in the following way: In thought and language there is a natural development from simple propositions to subject-predicate propositions, so that the concept which appears alone in the former type of proposition is combined with a second concept in the latter type of proposition, the second concept then serving as subject. Thus he writes (p. 25): "The subjectless propositions . . . are propositions which consist only of a predicate. In a great number of propositions, this predicate is to be thought of as being prior in the natural process of thought formation. It is then possible, though not at all necessary, to seek out some subject which may then be added to the predicate."

But this latter claim can hardly be correct; the word "subject", moreover, is not the one to use for the concept that may thus be added. Surely that which lays the basis for the judgement is what stands first in the construction of the judgement. The temporal sequence of words does not accord with what Miklosich says here, for normally we begin the categorical judgement with the subject. It is to be noted, moreover, that in categorical judgements the emphasis is usually upon the predicate. (This latter led Trendelenburg to describe the predicate as the principal concept and to say, with some exaggeration, "We think in predicates"; see Miklosich, p. 19.) If the subject concept, as Miklosich suggests, is the one that is added on to the concept that is first given, then we would hardly expect the predicate to be the object of greater interest; but if the predicate concept is the one that is added, then we would expect it to be of greater interest.

Where we say "A bird is black" we could also say "A black thing is a bird [*ein Schwarzes ist ein Vogel*]"; where we say "Socrates is a man", we could also say "Some man is Socrates". But Aristotle noted that only the former type of predication is natural, while the latter is opposed to the natural order. This is right insofar as we naturally take as the subject the term that we first consider when we make the judgement, or the term which the hearer must first attend to in order to understand the proposition or to find out whether or not it is true. If we wish to decide whether or not there is a black bird, we may look among birds to see whether there is one that is black, or we may look among black things to see whether there is one that is a bird, but it is preferable to take the former course. And if we wish to decide whether a given individual belongs to a certain genus or species, it is much easier to analyze the nature of that particular individual than it is to run through the extension of the relevant general concept. The apparent exceptions actually confirm the rule and the reasons that have been given for it. Suppose, for example, that I say: "There is a black thing; oh, the black thing is a bird." What I am aware of first in this case is simply a black thing, and therefore when I make a subject-predicate judgement it is natural for me to let the black thing be the subject.

In the Aristotelian sorites, the term that a premise has in common with its predecessor is taken to be the subject of that premise, but in the Goclenian sorites it is taken to be the predicate. For this reason, the Aristotelian sorites seems the more natural. It is said to exhibit the normal way of reasoning in a chain, whereas the Goclenian sorites reverses the normal order.

Again, consider what happens when we begin with a simple proposition, which does not combine a subject and predicate, and then proceed to a subject-predicate proposition in which one of the terms is the one that occurred in the simple proposition. Ordinarily, the term that is common to the two propositions would become the *subject* of the second proposition, and it would seem more natural to say that we have sought out a predicate for the subject than to say that we have sought out a subject for the predicate. For example: "There is noise; the noise comes from a brook"; "It is thundering; the thunder is a sign of an approaching storm"; "It smells of roses; the smell is coming from the neighbour's garden"; "There is laughter; the laughter comes from the clown"; "There is no money; the absence of money is the cause of the business depression"; "There is a God; this God is the creator of heaven and earth"; and so on.

It seems to me, therefore, that there is only *one* respect in which the expression "subjectless proposition" may be justified and perhaps even recommended. The expression takes account of the fact that the term which is contained in the propositions in question is the only term and therefore, obviously, the term which is of principal interest; and in propositions which have a subject and predicate the term which is of principal interest is the predicate and not the subject. Compare the relation that holds between categorical propositions and hypothetical propositions. If we had to choose, it would be much better to say that the categorical proposition is a "proposition without an antecedent" than to say that it is a "proposition without a consequent". But this would not mean that where there is no antecedent there may yet be a consequent; it means only that in a hypothetical proposition the consequent is the principal component. Looking at the matter this way, then, I might be able to go along with the author's "subjectless proposition".

But there is another point of disagreement. This concerns the extent to which we can make use of subjectless propositions. Miklosich is right in emphasizing that the limits must not be made too narrow. But he thinks that there *are* limits, as is shown by the fact that he attempts to survey and classify the sort of thing that can be expressed by these propositions. And here he seems to me to be mistaken. Strictly speaking, we may say that there is no limit to the applicability of the subjectless form. I think I have shown in my *Psychology* that *every* judgement, whether it be expressed in categorical, hypothetical, or disjunctive form, may be expressed without loss of meaning in the form of a subjectless proposition, or, as I would prefer to put it, in the form of an existential proposition. Thus the proposition "Some man is sick" is synonymous with "There is a sick man"; the proposition "All men are mortal" is synonymous with "There are no immortal men"; and so on.[1]

There is another respect in which what Miklosich has to say about the applicability of subjectless propositions would seem to be overly restrictive. He says that these propositions are "a great advantage to a language" and that "it is by no means true that all languages can boast of this advantage" (p. 26). But this is hardly plausible if, as he himself demonstrates so persuasively, there have always been judgements which are not formed by combining two different concepts, and which therefore cannot be expressed in subject-predicate form (p. 16). It follows that Miklosich is right when he says there are such things as subjectless propositions, and wrong when he says these propositions are not to be found in all languages.

I think that the author's mistake on this point may be traced in part to the fact that he was much too cautious. He wanted to be certain that his examples could not be objected to, and in consequence he leaves unmentioned certain types of subjectless

[1] Addendum: What I have said here about the general applicability of the existential form obviously is true only if we restrict ourselves to those judgements that are genuinely and perfectly unitary [einheitlich]. The tradition in logic is to express these judgements in categorical form, as subject-predicate propositions. But in ordinary life we often use the categorical, subject-predicate form to express a multiplicity of judgements, one built upon another. The proposition, "That is a man", is a clear example. Use of the demonstrative "that" already presupposes belief in the existence of the thing in question; a second judgement then ascribes to it the predicate "man". This happens very frequently. I would say that the original purpose of the categorical form was to express these double-judgements [Doppelurteilen]—judgements in which something is first accepted as existing and in which something else is then either affirmed or denied of the first thing. I would also say that existential and impersonal forms then grew out of this categorical form as a result of the change in function. But this fact does not alter their essential nature. Thus a lung is not a fish-bladder even if it did grow out of one. Again, the origin of the German preposition "kraft" ["by dint of"] may be traced to a substantive ["Kraft", meaning power]; nevertheless the word is syncategorematic and not a substantive (see Mill's Logic, Book I, Chapter 2, Section 2).

proposition. According to Miklosich, as we have already noted, the finite verb of subjectless propositions is always in the third person singular and, where differences in gender are utilized, it is always in the neuter. This is much too restrictive, and Miklosich himself has provided us with exceptions, though in a much later passage. He writes in the second part of his treatise: "In 'There is a God' the concept 'God' is asserted absolutely and without a subject; so, too, in 'There are gods'." And then he adds: "The 'is' of the existential proposition *takes the place of the so-called copula* 'is'. In many but by no means all languages, the so-called copula 'is' is indispensable for the expression of judgement and performs the same function as does the personal endings of finite verbs. We see this clearly when we consider 'It dawns' alongside of 'It is dawn'.* Consequently 'is' is not a predicate." (Page 34; compare also the top of page 21.) Actually, however, if *"Es gibt einen Gott"* is to be regarded as subjectless, then so, too, is *"Es ist ein Gott* [There is a God]" as well as *"Es sind Götter* [There are gods]". Hence the general rule that Miklosich sets up is too restrictive. If existential propositions (and possibly analogous forms) are subjectless prepositions, then this fact would confirm what we have said above—namely, that there are no languages, and cannot be any languages, in which these most simple of propositions are entirely absent. Miklosich says that some languages have advantages over others in providing for subjectless propositions; but this is true only of certain subspecies of these propositions.

These are the criticisms I have thought it necessary to make. But if they are found to be justified, they will not prejudice the author's principal theses in the slightest; indeed, they will add to the significance of what he says. The second edition of this small but substantial work, unduly neglected when it originally appeared, corrects certain points of detail, enlarges upon many points, and with great conciseness refutes the objections of Benfey, Steinthal, and other writers. Let me express once again my hope that it will find that interest which is appropriate to the importance of the question and to the excellent treatment that Miklosich has given it.

* [Translators' note: Miklosich's own examples are not adaptable to English; they are *"Es sommert, es nachtet"* and *"Es ist Sommer, es ist Nacht".*]

# APPENDIX
Drawn from Brentano's Letters and Manuscripts

## I. Ethical Principles as A Priori
### (From a letter to Oskar Kraus, March 24, 1904)

[Editor's note: On March 21st, 1904, I wrote to Brentano, making these points among others: "One thing has struck me in the course of my investigations. We call ourselves empiricists in ethics, but this is to be taken with a grain of salt. The concepts of *good* and *preferable* have their source in inner experience, in just the way in which the concept of *necessity* has its source in inner experience—and just as the concepts of *large* and *larger* have their source in so-called 'external experience'. But ethics is not based upon concepts; it is based upon certain *cognitions* (for example, the cognition that there can be no knowledge which, as such, is worthy of hate). These cognitions are acquired through consideration of the concepts that they presuppose. Hence they are 'analytic' or '*a priori*' in exactly the way in which the axioms of mathematics are 'analytic' or '*a priori*'. The only difference between the two cases is that the concepts of mathematics—those of geometry in particular—are 'ideal concepts' or fictions. Do you think that this is correct? And if not, why not?" The following is Brentano's reply.]

... A word about the question whether our point of view in ethics is to be called empirical. Obviously the answer depends upon the sense in which we take "empirical". There is no doubt but that we do get our ideas of good and of better from experience. But, as you rightly observe, the same is true of mathematics, and yet we do not on that account call mathematics an empirical science.

Now it is certain that the concept of *good* cannot be included in everything that is good; it is not included, for example, in the concept of knowledge. (Otherwise everything would include the concept of *good*, since everything contains some good.[1])

---

[1] [Editor's note: Brentano should be interpreted as referring here to beings that are psychologically active. Consider the man who is in excruciating pain: he is at least thinking, and he is aware of his own

"Knowledge is good" is not like the law of contradiction; the concepts, just by themselves, do not enable us to see that it is a true proposition. In this way it differs from the principles of mathematics; one *can* see, from the concepts alone, that two plus one is equal to three, for "two plus one" is the analytic definition of "three".

You note, however, that we also know, on the basis of concepts alone, that two plus one is *necessarily* equal to three, although the concept of *necessity* does not lie in the concept of two plus one. You are quite right. What happens in such cases is this: We combine three with two plus one by means of a negative copula, and then reject this combination apodictically. We are then led to concepts such as that of the *impossible* by reflecting upon the apodictic judgement. Thus there is an experience from which we derive such concepts as that of the *impossible*, and the object of this experience is the apodictic judgement.

It is in this way, then, that we arrive at the judgement, "It is necessarily true that two plus one is equal to three", despite the fact that the concept of "necessarily true" is not included in that of "two plus one". And this is quite different from the way in which we arrive at a generalization such as, "It is necessarily true that a physical body that is at rest will remain at rest unless it is disturbed by some other physical body, and that a physical body that is in motion will move in a straight line and with a uniform speed unless it is disturbed by some other physical body". In the case of the mathematical judgement, but not in the present case, the apodictic judgement, which provides the occasion for abstracting the concept of impossibility, arises out of the concepts alone. The ethical case is also unlike that of mathematics: the mere concept, "knowledge which is not good", does not provide the occasion for an apodictic rejection.

Thus still another experience is needed. The concept of knowledge must give rise to an act of love, and this love, just because it does arise in this way, is experienced as being correct. For a purely intellectual being, the thought that "two plus one is

---

existence and also of the fact that he is seeing or otherwise perceiving; to this extent, he is participating in what is good. Similarly for the man who is making a mistake and the man who is committing some criminal act.]

not equal to three" would be sufficient to give rise to its apodictic rejection; but (supposing, for the moment, that the concept of the good is given *a priori*)[2] the thought that "Knowledge is not good" would not give rise to apodictic rejection.

But the experience required is analogous to the one that we undergo upon contemplating, "It is impossible for two and one not to be equal to three". For the love that is experienced as being correct also arises out of concepts, and it is just because of this fact that the love is experienced as being correct. And so you are right in saying that this way of arriving at a generalization is quite different from what takes place when we make an induction. For where we have an induction in the strict and proper sense, as in the example above, we have only a probable generalization (in the most favourable case, one that is infinitely close to certainty). But in the ethical case, we have the absolute certainty of an apodictic judgement.

And so I think we should protest against calling this knowledge empirical—despite the fact that, in order to acquire the knowledge, it is necessary to feel and experience love. The knowledge that we have here is *a priori*. But when we say that a certain type of knowledge is *a priori*, we do *not* mean to imply that the concepts which it involves can be given without perception and apperception. What distinguishes the present type of *a priori* knowledge from the others is the fact that one must perceive and apperceive certain acts of *love* and not merely certain intellectual cognitions.

## II. *Decisions within the Sphere of the Emotions and the Formulation of the Supreme Moral Commandment*
(From a letter to Oskar Kraus, September 9, 1908)

Actually much of what I say in the *Ursprung sittlicher Erkenntnis* should be supplemented and perhaps also corrected.

The acts of loving and hating which are experienced as being correct are comparable to those apodictic judgements or truths of reason which are conceptually illuminating and also experienced

[2] [Editor's note: The supposition is essential since, in this fictional case, there would be no emotional experience from which the concept could be derived.]

as being correct; I did not take special note of this fact until after the publication of the *Ursprung*. These truths of reason, or axioms, as distinguished from perceptions that are directly evident, are occasioned, so to speak, by the concepts they illuminate (or, more exactly, by the thinker in so far as he is thinking these concepts). The emotions that are experienced as being correct arise from concepts in much the same way. The point would be obvious to any reader of the *Ursprung*, but it is important, and in taking explicit note of it we have made a step forward which is not without significance.

A second observation that I have subsequently made concerns a distinction between two types of emotional activity comparable to the distinction that Leibniz speaks of in connection with the will of God. There is the *volonté conséquente*, which always involves a decision, and there is the *volonté antécédente*, which does not. Thus I may love two things which are mutually exclusive; they are incompatible with each other in the sense that they cannot both be pursued simultaneously. Thus I may love doing sums and writing poetry, but on any particular occasion I can make a decision in favour of only one.

All acts of *will*, in the strict sense, consist of decisions. It is not possible to will incompatible things. And there are emotional activities other than willing which also involve decisions; these are activities having nothing to do with any practical good or evil. Thus I can decide that I want the weather to be good tomorrow, or that I would like to have a certain person come to visit, even though I can do nothing to bring these things about.

It might be suggested that what we are concerned with in such cases is nothing more than a matter of preference; but this is not correct. On the contrary, a man may have a rational preference which conflicts with some passionate desire; the desire may win out, with the result that one decides in favour of the desire, despite the rational preference. ("*Scio meliora proboque, deteriora sequor.*")

It now seems to me that ethics is concerned with such decisions in the sphere of the emotions [*Gemütsentscheidungen*]. It tells us that we must decide in accord with love that is experienced as being correct whenever such love is in conflict with our passions or with love that is not experienced as being correct.

In requiring that we make our decisions in this way, ethics

also tells us how by reflecting we are to prepare ourselves for such decisions in cases where the correctly qualified preference is not immediately given. We are to take note of what things considered in isolation are to be loved or to be hated, of what things are compatible with each other and what things not, and of what, under given conditions, is possible or impossible.

It is also a part of ethics to tell us how a correctly qualified love may be helped to overcome the passions and the like, to tell us about the formation of our general character (*Habitus*), and to teach us to seek out conditions that are favourable and to avoid those that are not.

There are still other things that I have subsequently done in ethics—for example, in connection with the value of a temporal process in which there is an ascent [from evil to good] as contrasted with one in which there is a descent, and in connection with the law of compensation [*Vergeltungsgesetz*], concerning which Leibniz makes some valuable observations in his *Theodicy*.[1] These things, for the most part, are well known to you and I will not discuss them now. I will turn, then, to your questions.

(1) You say that the precept "Choose the best that is attainable" is not always binding. I would answer that, because the precept is put in positive terms, we should say of it what moralists have long since established with respect to every positive command— namely, that it does not require fulfillment at every moment. Even "Love God above all and your neighbour as yourself", if we take it in the positive sense, is no exception. Otherwise we would not be permitted to sleep, for one cannot love God or one's neighbours while sleeping. But on the other hand, such

---

[1] [Editor's note: Brentano had made a number of subsequent observations in connection with the table of goods and evils. Thus the letter mentions the *malum regressus* involved in descent from a higher to a lower good, and the *bonum progressionis* involved in the ascent from a lower to a higher degree of perfection. According to the "law of compensation", a co-ordination of sensuous and other evils to moral evil may be a good. Brentano also came to hold, as Marty has noted, that whereas a whole is false if any one of its parts is false, "a sum may be worthy of love *as a whole* even though it is made up of goods and evils that balance each other off". See "Franz Brentano" in Anton Marty's *Gesammelte Schriften*, Vol. I (Halle: Max Niemeyer, 1916), pp. 97–103.]

precepts as "You must never decide against what God requires of you," and "You must never put any kind of pleasure before the fulfillment of the commands of God and of your own conscience", are altogether without exception.

But the precept "Choose the best that is attainable" can also be taken negatively, as saying "Never choose anything less than the best that is attainable", and then it holds entirely without exception.

I think you might find it interesting to compare some good Catholic moralist, perhaps St. Thomas himself, with respect to this distinction between positive and negative commands. Perhaps the doubts which trouble you now would then disappear completely.

(2) You say that the supreme ethical duty is that of willing correctly. Willing, as you conceive it, is a broader concept than that of choosing, but you do speak of a will which is faced with a question. Isn't the question which is thus addressed to the will at least one that Hamlet raised—"To be or not to be"? If so, the decisions of the will would be a matter of choosing, after all. But even for me, as you will gather from what is said above, *deciding*, in the sphere of the emotions, is a broader concept than that of *choosing*. Deciding goes beyond the sphere of the will itself, for it may include wishing, and my wishes may pertain to that which I cannot help to bring about or to prevent.

It should be noted that what I have said about the distinction between positive and negative commands also holds for the precept, "Will correctly". This is not a positive command, requiring that one always will correctly, for one cannot be perpetually engaged in willing.

## III. The Relativity of Secondary Moral Laws[1]

*Schönbühel bei Melk a. d. Donau,*
*September 2, 1893*

To the Editor:

You ask whether I think that a person is ever justified in taking his own life. My respect for your paper compels me to reply, even though I cannot add anything to what has already been long known.

[1] [Editor's note: This brief letter, which Brentano wrote for the

THE RELATIVITY OF SECONDARY MORAL LAWS

If a man is still able to base his decisions upon considerations that pertain to good and evil, and the question is significant only to the extent that it pertains to such a man, then, without doubt, his life is something that is good. But it is not the highest good. Generally speaking, suicide is to be condemned. But there is one situation in which suicide is not only permissible, but is also an act of virtue—namely, when a good yet higher than one's own life is in jeopardy. Rebecca, in Walter Scott's "Ivanhoe", decides to throw herself into the abyss rather than to fall into the hands of the Templar; in so doing, she has the sympathy of the author and of any morally sensitive reader. And according to the most distinguished theologians, the Christian Church itself, though it forbids suicide in general, refuses to condemn the virgin who takes her life in order not to be dishonoured.

Like any other secondary moral rule, the rule forbidding suicide permits exceptions. The only rule having unconditional, universal validity is the basic moral law—the law telling us that there are no circumstances under which we may choose anything in preference to the highest good.

Here, too, what I say is in accord with the teachings not only of the most advanced science but also of that religion which for

editor of the *Deutsche Zeitung* in Vienna (September 6, 1893), is concerned with the relation that secondary or derivative moral laws bear to the one supreme moral law. Perhaps it would not be superfluous to anticipate an objection. I have often heard it said that there are, quite obviously, many unexceptionable moral laws; for example, "One must not commit murder" and "One must not lie" are universally binding and permit no exceptions. But this is to overlook the fact that such expressions as "murder", "steal", and "lie" are what Bentham called "dyslogistic". That is to say, they are expressions which already classify the deed in question as one that is wrong. A "murder" is a killing that is wrong; one tells a "lie" if one wrongly utters a falsehood. And so the real question becomes: is it in *all* circumstances wrong to kill, or to utter a falsehood, or to take over the property of another? And the answer is this: experience tells us that for the most part such acts are wrong and therefore that they are to be avoided as a general rule. But "One must not kill" is a secondary rule, since it allows for the possibility that some killings are justified. "One must not commit murder", on the other hand, is restricted in its application to those killings that are not justified, thus telling us only that unjustified killing is always wrong.]

117

centuries has been professed by the most advanced peoples—a religion that is ethically superior to all the others known to history. Christianity knows only *one* immediate supreme commandment, and it is this one commandment which gives validity to all the others. "Upon it depends the law and all the prophets."[2]

Under what circumstances, then, has a man the right to take his own life? It would be too much for me or any other moralist to try to enumerate them. Anyone with a good imagination could think of innumerable cases. But to make the general point clearer, I will add one example.

Suppose that a man has been entrusted with secret information and that the well-being of his countrymen depends upon his not divulging it. Suppose that he falls into the hands of the enemy; he knows that they will submit him to the most horrible of tortures in order to get the information and he is morally certain that he will not have the strength to withstand them. If such a man takes his life for the sole purpose of saving his country from ruin, I would not even think of condemning him morally. I would say instead that he deserves our admiration for his patriotism. And I suspect that there are very few who would disagree with me.

Let me add just one point in conclusion. Even if, generally speaking, suicide is morally blameworthy, it does not follow that the state should institute punishments for those who attempt it. If a man is prepared to take his own life, then he will hardly be deterred by the threat of any punishment that the state might inflict. After all, the state considers the death penalty to be the most extreme punishment that there is. . . .

## IV. Punishment and its Justification

*1* Why does the state punish people for breaking laws? Because only the threat of punishment assures, or makes probable, compliance.

*2* Hence the reason for establishing punitive measures is the same as the reason for issuing penal laws.

[2] [Editor's note: Compare Brentano's *Die Lehre Jesu und ihre bleibende Bedeutung*.]

*3* The most essential concern of the state is to safeguard the rights of property, life, honour, and the like; the protection of these goods is also the primary purpose of the criminal code.

*4* And therefore this concern must also determine the means of punishment.

*5* Given the purpose of punishment, two considerations should determine the severity of the measures to be used. These are: (1) the gravity of the wrong to be prevented; and (2) the probability that only the fear of very great punishment will be sufficient to deter people from breaking the law, and that a lesser punishment will be ineffectual.

*6* But the calculations are not quite so simple. In determining its punitive laws, the state must also take into account the cases in which laws are broken *despite* the threat of punishment. If such cases did not occur, if it were possible to prevent transgressions universally and with certainty by means of draconic legislation, stipulating the most ghastly punishment for every violation, then this practice, which is condemned as inhuman, would be the one to follow. In fact, however, the consequences of criminal law are these: (1) in some cases, violation of the law is prevented; (2) in other cases, in which the law is broken despite the threat of punishment, punishment is inflicted; and (3) in still other cases, crimes are committed but concealed.

*7* The second case demands particularly careful consideration.

*8* The punishment adds still another ill to that of the crime itself. It places restrictions upon the person being punished and in many cases does him serious harm. The restraints lead to suffering; there is exile, imprisonment, degradation, mutilation. The more severe the punishment, the greater the injury. And the injury can be so great that the infliction of punishment is itself wrong even if it succeeds in securing general compliance. In such cases the state is transgressing against the moral law.

Furthermore, even if the state has as little desire as the individual to avenge the evil act, it certainly must take into account the degree of reprisal that is appropriate to the deed. The punishment should never be disproportionately severe. There are also proper limits to protection, not only for the individual but also for the state. If someone wants to steal my apple and I kill him because that is the only way I can stop him, I have far exceeded these bounds. The state would also exceed them if it were to threaten capital punishment in order to safeguard my possession of the apple.

The principle aim of the state is to protect property.[1] But the legal order itself is merely a secondary ethical principle; only the primary principle is valid without exception. Thus the state has a general duty to safeguard property, but in particular cases deference to the primary ethical law, which is called for at all times, may forbid the state to do what it is generally required to do. Then the moral law will set certain limits to the activity of the state, as indeed it always does, and may even curtail it completely.

*9* Given these principles, it is possible to explain what many people have found incomprehensible. Many have despaired of finding the connection between the state's threats of punishment and the idea of protection. Why is it, they have wondered, that much milder punishments are allotted when greater temptations are present, even though these are the cases in which the law is most vulnerable to violations?

The answer is this: (1) a lesser degree of punishment is called for, and, as already noted, the proper boundaries may not be overstepped; (2) the people in question are relatively good, and the restraint and injury of such persons is less to be desired; and (3) the wrong produced by unbounded punishment would be the more regrettable, since the degree of temptation increases the number of infractions.

*10* Consideration of the cases in which violation is concealed (see the third point at the end of paragraph 6) readily makes it clear that such concealment would become more common if unduly severe punishments were instituted. For in such cases, not only the guilty person, but other people, too, would be con-

[1] [Editor's note: "Property" is to be taken here in its broadest sense.]

cerned to prevent the authorities from knowing of the deed, and this concern would proceed from motives that are normally justified. And this, of course, would be detrimental to the aims of penal legislation in general.

*11* Protection, then, is the proper motive for establishing a criminal code. And there is no glaring conflict, as some have thought, between this purpose and our actual practice.

*12* One should not suppose, of course, that our practice is ideal or that it is guided by a clear knowledge of the reasons which ought to determine it. Nevertheless, these reasons unmistakably exert an influence. The fact that retribution ought to be taken into account has misled some into making revenge the essence of the penal law, something quite out of keeping with that sublime passage from the Holy Scriptures: "Vengeance is mine."

*13* In instituting punishment, it is essential to take the following factors into consideration, among others. (a) The punishment should not be such that, though it is objectively the same for different offenders, it will be subjectively different.[2] (b) And the suffering which is the evil concomitant of punishment should be incurred so as to interfere as little as possible with the performance of good actions. Sometimes it is possible to inflict this suffering in such a way that either the offender himself or certain other persons will, in consequence, be able to do more good than they otherwise would have done. And this, quite obviously is the arrangement to be preferred, all other things being equal.

*14* It is also important to determine the extent to which the severity of punishment should be a function of the probability that certain crimes will be concealed. Clearly threats are less effective when concealment is possible; the effectiveness is directly proportional to the probability of discovery. An increase in the severity may be permissible and advisable in these cases. But the severity should not exceed the bounds of suitable retribution. It would be a fiction, and one to be condemned as unjust, to view all offenders

[2] [Editor's note: Brentano probably means that the punishment should be suited to the particular circumstances of the offender.]

as though they were conjointly responsible for crimes that are individually committed.

*15* Suppose that a thief has been punished and that the degree of punishment was suitable as retribution. Is it then permissible to go beyond this retribution and require him to make restitution? And may further injury be inflicted upon him to prevent him from stealing again? It can hardly be right thus to exceed the retribution that is called for. And what we have here is not *punishment*, in the strict sense of the term. People have sometimes spoken of *"legibus mere poenalibus"*. In such cases, there is no guilt and therefore no retribution is called for. But should there be such laws? Does not the very concept of such a law contain the confession of an unjustified imposition?

*16* Other unjust demands are sometimes made. The maxim, *"Salus rei publicae suprema lex"*, is in itself immoral. It leads to unjust laws and therefore also to unjust punishment.

Self-preservation is not the highest principle of the state. Under certain circumstances the state is obligated to aim at its own dissolution. It should surrender without resistance, even in the face of unjust attacks, if defence is hopeless or requires too great a sacrifice on the part of its citizens. It must not be forgotten that the state is not itself the supreme end. The state is only a means to higher goods. And when these are sacrificed in order to preserve the state, then the proper order of things is reversed.

## V. Epicurus and the War[1]

An article with the above title was recently published in the *Internationale Rundschau*. In stressing the fact that the craving for war cannot be condoned under any circumstances, even from the standpoint of extreme egoism, it has my complete approval.[2] The author is fully aware of the folly of viewing the state as an

[1] [Editor's note: This article first appeared in the Zurich *Internationale Rundschau*, January 15, 1916.]

[2] [Editor's note: Brentano was a decided pacifist and thought it madness to allow questions of international justice to be decided by the fortunes of war.]

entity over and above particular individuals, as though it were a higher being for whose welfare lesser creatures should sacrifice their lives and possessions. He knows how absurd it is to suppose that it is better for a whole people to be robbed of its happiness and to be subjected to unspeakable suffering than it is for the state to fail to maintain itself in full power or even to cease to extend its power. This species of madness, which is all too common at the present time, contains a most peculiar reversal of the proper order of means and end. Surely the state exists for man, not man for the state. The state exists only as a means; it is not good in itself. That patriotism which goes so far as to reverse this order cannot be admired as a virtue; we should rather condemn it as a moral error, similar to that of the miser who sacrifices his personal happiness to the collecting of riches as though this activity were something that is truly good, if not one of the higher goods.

The author is to be commended for having stressed once again a truth which so many fail to recognize in our time. But it is most regrettable that in condemning these excesses from the standpoint of the egoist, he accuses the proponents of theism of originating or encouraging them. He does not produce anything even vaguely resembling a proof of the latter claim, unless it be this: that any theory assuming the existence of a divine principle goes beyond the bounds of experience and is therefore pure nonsense or, as the author puts it, totally irrational. He finds it not surprising that those who can blunder into such absurdities are also capable of making a fetish of the state.

In referring contemptuously to *all* theistic thinkers, the author shows that he is not at home with the history of philosophy. If he were, he would know that in both ancient and modern times precisely the most important thinkers and those who were most acute have been theists: Anaxagoras, Plato, Aristotle, Descartes, Locke, Leibniz. In some ways, even Kant who is now so highly esteemed, should be counted as a theist, despite his view that the transcendent is incapable of investigation. And Albert Lange, the author of the *Geschichte des Materialismus*, was compelled to admit that we are indebted solely to spiritualists, and not to materialists, for the great discoveries in the exact sciences that were made in ancient times. Similarly, Romanes, the Darwinian psychologist, marvelled at the fact that almost all of the English investigators among his contemporaries who were especially noted for their mathematical acuity—for example, Maxwell, Lord Kelvin, and a great many of the better-known Cambridge professors—were convinced theists. In order to see that the same is true of great scientific thinkers in Germany, one need only mention Johannes Müller, Liebig, Schwann, Pflüger, and Helmholtz. The author's proof, which was bad enough to begin with, falls completely apart in the face of such facts as these.[3]

It is most regrettable, moreover, that in the practical interests of peace, one of its friends should make insulting attacks upon others, for this can only result in dispersing forces at a time it is most important to hold them together. Franklin, in trying to bring together all those who strive to do the good into one association, which he called the "Society of the Doers of Good", offered us an example of the kind of tolerance for which we are pleading; he took no offence at even the greatest differences of opinion. The intolerance of the present author becomes obvious when we consider that during our time almost no one has worked with greater zeal at restoring peace than Benedict XV, the head of the Catholic Church.

In spirit, Christianity has always been a religion of peace and it is so today, even if, time and again, the stupidity of mankind has led to wars that have been waged, supposedly, in the interests of religion. The folly of those who advocate an egoistic morality leads even more readily to war. Certainly the roots of our present ills lie in egoistical impulses and not in religious convictions. I could easily show that this is true. I could also show that if anyone is to be charged with having an irrational philosophy, it should be the followers of Epicurus and not those who are theists. Epicurus, perhaps more than any other philosopher, showed himself to be completely superficial. But for me to go further into these matters would be to fall into the kind of intolerance against which I have been protesting—an intolerance toward those who are one with me in loving peace.

[3] [Editor's note: Cf. Brentano, "Der Atheismus und die Wissenschaft", published anonymously in *Historisch-politische Blätter f. d. katholische Deutschland*, Vol. 2 (1873), pp. 852 and 916.]

*VI. The Young Benjamin Franklin's Attack upon Ethics*
(later emphatically repudiated but without insight
into the logical error involved)[1]

I

*1* Morality, it is generally supposed, requires us to inform
ourselves in as much detail as possible concerning the relative
value of the things among which we must choose and then to give
preference to what is better, and to do so *because* it is better. The
conscientious man will proceed with care and often at considerable sacrifice to himself.

*2* But all this seems absurd in the light of the most sublime of
philosophical truths. There is a God and he is infinitely good,
infinitely wise, and infinitely powerful. Nothing can happen unless it has been infallibly foreseen and arranged through divine
providence and unless it is predetermined to bring about the best
possible end in the most perfect way.

*3* Consequently everything that does happen must be acknowledged as being without doubt—then and there, at the time at
which it occurs—the best possible means for the best possible
end.

*4* But in that case what is the point of moral deliberation and
self-sacrifice? Why shouldn't each man indulge himself as he
pleases without any qualms of conscience at all? For whatever
harm the indulgence may *seem* to threaten, this appearance will
prove deceptive once the agent succeeds in bringing about what
he has undertaken. For what has just been said of *every* event will
also hold of his particular act: as a part of the divine world-plan
it is precisely what is required at that time and place for bringing
about the best that is possible. It is only our own limited per-
spective that prevents us from surveying the whole network of
relations and giving an account of how and by what means each

[1] [Editor's note: Franklin speaks of this attack in his *Autobiography*.
Brentano attempted to put the thought as precisely as possible and
did not use Franklin's own words. This piece was written sometime
before 1901.]

125

event occurs. Given that the agent has undertaken the act without any reflection and without sacrificing himself in any way, then it is only if he does *not* succeed, and to the extent that he does not succeed, that he may properly be said to have undertaken something which is not the best means to the best end.

*5* What is the consequence of this? If what we set out to do without any probing of conscience is something that is *not* the best possible deed in just those circumstances, then it is something that we cannot possibly succeed in doing! Clearly *this* type of failure will do no harm at all to what is good or to what is best.

Whoever is unaware of this may have as many scruples as he likes and deny himself as often as he pleases. But whoever does know it—as we do, thanks to our philosophical deliberations— is released from all moral bonds, even if he does love what is good and what is to be preferred. Given this awareness, we would seem to be free of any type of moral reproach. Do what you wish and have no misgivings at all! That is the final word of the most sublime practical wisdom.

## II

The young Benjamin Franklin, then, has given us an argument purporting to show that the belief in a God who is infinitely good, wise, and powerful, and in his predetermination of everything that occurs, is sufficient to produce moral paralysis in any consistent thinker.

To indicate briefly what is wrong with this argument, I will show (1) that the conclusion is false and (2) why the argument is not sound. Franklin saw the first point himself, but he confessed that the second always remained a mystery to him.

(1) It is easy to see that the conclusion is false. To the extent to which an agent in a given set of circumstances can foresee the results of his actions and then give preference to that which promises to bring about the greater amount of good, he will in fact produce a greater amount of good, generally speaking, than he would by acting merely upon impulse. This is just a point of good sound reason—which here, as elsewhere, is confirmed by the calculus of probability. (So far as the unforeseeable consequences of the two ways of acting are concerned, the probabilities are the same on both sides and therefore, according

YOUNG BENJAMIN FRANKLIN'S ATTACK UPON ETHICS

to the law of large numbers, these consequences, generally speaking, would come out the same. Hence the difference with respect to the predictable consequences will tip the scale in favour of the act which proceeds from deliberation.) The result of such forethought and deliberation is most significant in the case of those agents who have the greatest amount of insight and who therefore are best able to foresee the results of their actions and to determine correctly the value of the various goods and evils involved and then to choose the most suitable means for bringing about what is good. But if Franklin's argument were sound, then the most perceptive among those who believe in God's predetermination would be led to choose and to act without any thought about the goodness or badness of what they do. In consequence these people would bring about less good than others and the result therefore would be as it should be—which is contrary to the claims of the argument.

(2) What, then, is wrong with Franklin's argument? The answer is this:

Some *preferences* may be said to have a moral character and others not.

The preference of one object over another is a preference that has *moral character* if the agent takes the one object to be *better* than the other.[2] His preference is moral if he favours what he believes to be better because he believes it to be better; his preference is immoral when he favours the opposite.

A preference is *without* moral relevance, on the other hand, when the agent believes that the objects in question are of equal value or when he finds himself unable to make any judgement about the preferability of the one or the other. And what has been said about preference in general also holds of what may be

[2] [Editor's note: Taking one object to be better than another is what is sometimes called making a judgement of value. More exactly, it is making a judgement of *preference*—arriving at a conviction which is based upon a preference that is experienced as being correct. The type of preference that is here under discussion, as Brentano goes on to observe, is a "preferential choosing and willing" which is based upon such a conviction. Those emotive acts which are experienced as being correct and which are presupposed by our judgements of value are not themselves acts of will; they are emotive acts that arise out of the concepts that are involved.]

127

called practical preference; that is to say, it also holds of acts of choice. For choosing is simply preferential willing.

(Not every act of preference is an act of choosing. The agent may also have a preference with respect to two incompatible things which he believes to be outside the sphere of his own influence. For instance, he may wish that the sun would shine and thus *prefer* the sun to rain, but there is no act of *choice* in such a case.)

Now what holds generally of acts of choice also holds of the choices that are made by those people who believe in divine providence and in God's unlimited power of predetermination.

What must we show, then, if we are to prove that the choices that such people make are without moral relevance? We must show one or the other of two things: either (a) that the people, if they are to be rational and consistent, must take the objects among which they choose to be of equal value; or (b) that in the situations involved it is impossible to form a reasonable judgement having any degree of certainty or probability.

But the doctrine of divine providence and predetermination does not imply either of these things.

It does not imply that the objects among which choices are to be made are all of equal value. To be sure, it follows from the doctrine that every event is a *part* of the best possible ordering of means to the best possible end, but not that all such parts are themselves of equal value. And indeed it is not the case that all such parts are all of equal value.[3] But Franklin is committed to saying that they are, since, according to him, the doctrine implies that each event is itself the best possible means to the best possible end. And this is quite wrong. A thing is a means only for whatever it is that the thing brings about.

If a thing is to be itself the means to the best possible end, then it must produce the best possible of all the effects that can be pro-

---

[3] [Editor's note: In a note on the manuscript, Brentano remarks that one must hold unequivocally to the proposition that every event is a *part* of the best possible means for the best possible end. From this it will follow that each event is ordered in the best possible way in relation to the best possible end. But, as Brentano goes on to say in the passage above, it does not follow that each individual event is *itself* the best possible means to the best possible end.]

duced. But no such claim can be made for any single event in the world; no single event is itself the cause of the entire universe. And it is the entire universe that is the best possible end. The particular events in the universe serve ends of various sorts. These particular events, quite obviously, do not all have the same value in themselves, nor are their various effects of equal value.

The latter point bears directly upon what was said in connection with (1) above. Of the various events that are within my power (and among which I must make a choice) there may be one which, generally speaking, would bring about a greater amount of good than any of the others; this will be the one which is best in its foreseeable effects. Therefore it is not true that one who believes in divine providence and predetermination is unable to make any probable judgements about the value of the possible courses of action that are open to him.

And so, for such a person, neither of the conditions which would deprive choice of its moral relevance can be said to hold. Hence Franklin was not justified in concluding that a consistent person would be morally paralyzed if he were to believe in divine providence and predetermination.[4]

[4] [Editor's note: At least this much truth is contained in Franklin's thought: our misdeeds do not endanger the best possible that God can produce; they endanger only the best possible that we can produce. One must keep in mind the fact that the so-called omnipotence of God consists in his being able to do everything that is *possible*; it does not mean that he can produce what is in itself impossible. He cannot make the past become the present or make two and two equal to five. Now if a world that is free of impropriety and misdeeds is in itself impossible, then God must produce events (for example, criminal acts of will) the evil character of which is to be viewed as a condition *sine qua non* for that which is the best possible that he can produce. That which is the best possible, for the most perfect cause, can only be the unending ascent of the entire spiritual creation to ever greater perfection; here the universe is not to be thought of as restricted to the three-dimensional spatial manifold, for there are types of spatial object (e.g., topoids having dimensions that are unknown to us) which are inaccessible to our experience but which can be thought without contradiction.]

## VII. On the Moral Perfection of the First Cause of All Contingent Beings[1]

There are three ways by which men come to know that there is a substance which is necessary in itself and which creates all other beings. (1) Motion requires a first cause that is itself uncaused. This first cause is a creative as well as a moving principle. It possesses powers which stand in no finite relation to the powers of such beings as ourselves; it is a substance of infinite reality. (2) The proof based upon the contingency of those substances which lie within our own experience leads in a similar way to the same conclusion. (3) And, finally, if we consider the apparent purposiveness of the various phenomena falling within our experience and if we ask ourselves whether these are produced by an intelligent being or whether they have come about merely by accident (the hypothesis of blind necessity is obviously unacceptable), we are led to assume the existence of a principle which not only orders the universe but which creates also all beings other than itself. Here, too, the infinite reality of such a being is beyond doubt. And it is easy to prove that this infinite substance is infinitely superior to every created thing, in its knowledge and in its intellect.[2] But some people who are certain of the infinite power and knowledge of this world principal have serious doubts about its *moral* character. The existence of suffering and of ignorance, the moral depravity of men, and the fact that the goods and evils of this world are not justly distributed—these things are taken to show that the creator and ruler of the world *cannot* be infinitely good if he is infinitely powerful.

Theodicy can easily demonstrate that this last attack is unsound. But it is one thing to refute those who claim to prove that the world cannot be the work of a being that is infinitely good, and it is quite another thing to show with any degree of plausibility that the author of the world *is* morally perfect. A morally perfect being would favour what is to be preferred just because of the fact that it is to be preferred. But without limited knowledge of the world, we are hardly able to compare other

[1] [Editor's note: This essay was written some time close to 1906.]
[2] [Editor's note: Compare Brentano's *Vom Dasein Gottes* (Leipzig: Felix Meiner, 1929), ed. Alfred Kastil.]

possible world-orders with this one; we are not in a position, therefore, to prove directly that the characteristics of this world are such as to make it the best possible. Even Leibniz had to concede this point. The only conceivable way of showing that this is the best possible world is to give an indirect demonstration: on the basis of the empirical facts that are available to us, we must show that the world emanates from a being that is infinitely perfect; and *then* we can deduce, indirectly, that the world-order which such a being would choose must be the best one that is possible. Let us proceed in this manner.

Some of the creatures within our experience are rational beings. We find these beings to be equipped with the knowledge of good and bad, of the better and the less good, of the duty to prefer the better to the worse, and therefore of the duty to prefer, so far as their knowledge and power permit, the best that is possible. People often behave contrary to duty, but never without an internal struggle. Their conscience, as we say, condemns them and admonishes them. Dissatisfaction with themselves often gives rise to violent sensuous displeasure. Poets speak of the furies who persecute those who have bad consciences. All this is to be traced back to the first world principle as creator and arranger. It is clear that he himself has knowledge of the good and approves of it, for he gives to the highest creatures the assignment of loving what is good and of always giving preference to what is better. The fact that the creature does not fully live up to this assignment and, indeed, that the majority are far from living an ideal moral life should not dissuade us from the conviction that we do have such a calling. Although each blossom is surely called upon to bear fruit, very few actually serve to propagate their kind. Throughout all nature, many are called and few are chosen. We may readily confirm this by surveying the order of things in the world. Why should it not also be true within the moral realm? Consider, then, the being who gave this moral assignment to the creatures that are most like him. Surely he must himself, be endowed to an infinite degree, with moral knowledge and with a moral will. Since he is an infinite being, who lacks no reality, it can hardly be supposed that he would himself be subject to moral weakness.

If we consider further the analogy between him and created rational beings, we realize that, if he were not morally perfect, then he would not be at peace with himself and could never be truly free and omnipotent. Though he bestows happiness upon the good in the greatest moments of their lives, he would lack it himself. And despite the power that he is able to exert over others, there is a sense in which he would be lamentably powerless with respect to himself. He would be unable to appease his unceasing desire for moral perfection. He could lead the created sinner to conversion, but he would be unable to free himself from his own immoral condition, which he would recognize with infinite clarity. Is it not monstrous, then, to suppose that the principle of the world might not be morally perfect?

These observations may be confirmed if we consider the way in which created beings may come to hate the good and to favour the less good over what they know to be better. How could anything as strange and unreasonable as this come to be? Indeed one is inclined to suppose, *a priori*, that it cannot really happen—that it is impossible because it is contradictory. But it does happen, and we can explain it in the following way.

(1) Within the sphere of judgement, we find that we are equipped not only with the power of making judgements that are insightful but also with an impulse to form judgements that are blind. In forming such judgements, we are guided by the creator's understanding. The judgements may be unreasonable in themselves, but they perform an important function for us; indeed, without them, we would not acquire any knowledge at all. Think of the instinctive impulse to trust external perception, of the instinctive faith that we have in our memory, and of the expectations that we come to have as a result of habit—expectations that are quite different from those rational beliefs that are based upon the calculus of probability. The sphere of the emotions is analogous in these respects to the sphere of judgement. Nature has given us the ability to feel love and preference that is experienced as being correct. And it has given us emotions that are blind. Thus feelings of sensuous pleasure and displeasure are blind emotions that lead us astray in many ways. They make us avoid some things that we do not know to be bad and they lead us to other things that we do not know to be good. And our instinct is so blind that we will do this without having any knowledge or even any presentiment about the things in question. This limitation—the fact that we are subject to drives that

are blind as well as to love that is experienced as being correct—has the following consequences. (a) We may come to hate in itself something which in fact is to be hated only because of something else; thus we come to have an emotion that is incorrect. And (b) some of these blind passions may come into conflict with a love that is experienced as being correct; the passions may prove to be so powerful that we are reduced to preferring what in fact we ought to reject; and then we act in a way that is contrary to our better knowledge and desire. If these passions have been unduly favoured in the past, then they become more and more likely to exert a strong influence in the present. A morally depraved character is formed only after long years of habituation.

And now let us consider, once again, the eternal and infinite spirit and compare him with such beings of limited rationality. It is clear that habit can have no influence upon him. He is able to choose throughout all eternity. Where there is unlimited knowledge instead of limited vision, it would be absurd to suppose that there is anything like blind passion in addition to love that is experienced as being correct. An infinite being would have no need of such aids.

(2) When a finite being prefers a lesser good, he may be following an egoistical drive. Such drives will allow a subordinate goal to come into conflict with the absolute goal. One could say, in fact, that every creature is provided by nature with certain virtues that are appropriate to its own condition; and these virtues may not do justice to all the distinctions of value holding among the objects with which the creature is concerned. This arrangement is justified because of the way in which it works out in its details. But nothing of this sort can be true of the first world principle. His subjective goal *is* the objective goal. If God loves himself above all else, then his love is correct. If an omniscient being can come to gain anything, it is by experiencing a more perfect act of knowing whenever there comes into being a greater perfection to be known. If he loves his own perfection to the highest degree, and his own knowledge and joy, then his love will coincide perfectly with the preference of what is better and of what is the best of everything that is possible. In loving what is more perfect, he loves what is more like himself; this is true of us, as it is of him. Would God be capable of receiving an

injury or some minor benefit from some creature that is better than himself—and whom he therefore refrains from creating? This would be out of the question. God is not subject to *any* influence from without—either harmful or beneficial. He acts but he is not acted upon. There is no need to spell out the absurdity of supposing otherwise. The most perfect being could hardly be injured by a creature that is even more perfect. And how could he be said to choose what is to be preferred if he were to choose what would bring harm to an infinitely perfect good— that is to say, to the author of all creation? The first principle of the world is to be thought of as infinite in substance, knowledge, and power, and infinite in respect to its desire, will, and choice. For this reason (and only for this reason) it is also to be considered infinite in its inner peace and blessedness.

## *VIII. Happiness and Unhappiness*[1]

Everyone has something to say about happiness and unhappiness. In dealing with a topic of such great generality, we will do well to consider the views of ordinary men along with those of the greatest and the wisest of thinkers.

But the two sets of views are very far apart. The great majority of people speak of happiness and unhappiness as though they were external forces which hold us in their power.

The wise man knows, however, that happiness and unhappiness are entirely independent of the external situation of the subject. Two men in the same external situation need not be equally happy or equally unhappy. Indeed we may find that one man is happy in just those circumstances in which another man is unhappy.

[1] [Editor's note: This little essay is not dated. There is no indication in the handwriting, which is Brentano's own, of diminishing eyesight; it must have been written, therefore, before he became blind and in all probability before 1903, the year of his first operation for cataracts. As a true philosopher, Brentano endured his affliction, not only with the kind of patient resignation that he speaks of here, but also with serenity. An excellent indication of this latter is his little book of riddles, *Aenigmatias*, which first appeared in 1878 and for which Brentano prepared a second edition in 1909. [The fifth edition was published by Francke Verlag, Bern and Munich, 1962.]]

## HAPPINESS AND UNHAPPINESS

And therefore Heraclitus taught that happiness and unhappiness depend entirely upon one's inner disposition:

Τὸ ἦθος ἀνθρώπῳ δαίμων.

The situation as Heraclitus views it is like that described in recent works on the psychology of sensation: the qualities that our sensations have depend more upon the nature of the nervous system than upon that of their external stimuli.

We must not deny, however, that certain occurrences, by their very nature, tend to give us pleasure and that others naturally tend to give us pain.

Thus there are some occurrences that we call pleasant and agreeable, and others we call unpleasant and disagreeable; some we call beautiful and others we call ugly. And there are morally ugly phenomena which the high-minded man looks upon with distaste.

We should make this concession to the common man, therefore: he is perfectly right when he speaks of happy and unhappy occurrences. But we should insist at the same time that much depends upon the way in which we react to these occurrences. For whether or not an unhappy occurrence—a misfortune—will make us unhappy is something that depends upon us. As one of the wise men of ancient Greece has put it:

ἀτυχής ἐστιν ὁ ἀτυχίαν μὴ φέρων.

What, then, is the proper attitude to take towards a misfortune if we are to keep it from making us unhappy?

Obviously, it is essential to distinguish between two quite different types of case: in one, there is something that can be done about the misfortune itself; in the other, there is nothing that can be done, or at least nothing that we ourselves can do.

In the former case, the proper course is to take up arms against the misfortune and do what one can to overcome it. The effort may turn bad fortune into good, and we may take pleasure and consolation at the very outset in our courage and hope.

But in the latter, where it is not possible or not permissible to do anything about the unfortunate event itself, how are we to prevent it from causing us unhappiness? There are those who would advise us to try to put it out of mind:

"Glücklich ist,
Wer vergisst,
Was nicht mehr zu ändern ist."

APPENDICES

["Happy is the man who can forget what cannot be altered."]
What we are told to do, in short, is to conceal the truth and
to deceive ourselves.

It would be most unfortunate if this were the only way in
which we could prevent ourselves from being unhappy. For
knowledge is clearly something good, and self-deception is, as
such, an evil and a kind of degradation. The wise man, therefore, takes another course: a resigned and patient acceptance of
the facts. Patient resignation is a virtue; far from being a matter
of deception or ignorance, it is inconceivable without knowledge
of a noble and lofty kind, even if it is not itself knowledge.

We can best appreciate what this resignation is if we contrast
it with its opposite. A person who is impatient angrily resists
whatever is disagreeable to him; he will try to get rid of it when
he cannot succeed, or when he can succeed only by creating an
evil that is greater than the one he overcomes. Thus the prisoner
yanks with indignation at his chains; the man who cannot get
the window open smashes it instead; the man who tries without
success to correct a minor error impatiently gives up the entire
endeavour; and the short-tempered teacher renounces his pupil.
The man who is waiting for his friend paces up and down and
keeps turning his head toward the place from which he expects
the friend to come, as though all of this could somehow hasten
the arrival. In these cases, we have a battle without a victory,
or a partial victory at the expense of an overall defeat.

In each case, the end result is an increase in sorrow and suffering. The man who is forever fighting and losing keeps alive the
misery of defeat. And whoever sacrifices the greater good makes
the total situation worse instead of better. Such a man may
accomplish something, but his procedure is hardly wise, for he
adds to sorrow and suffering as a result of what he overlooks,
be it the nature of what he is sacrificing or simply the fact that he
cannot succeed.

One may also act unwisely even without resisting what cannot
be avoided: one may persist in longing for what cannot be had.
The possession of what is good is a source of pleasure, but the
desire for it is a source of pain. Indeed, Epicurus advised his
followers to avoid all desires. Everyone agrees that our desires
should not be so strong that they force out the thought of everything else. When we temper our desires, we find, moreover,

that other goods remain and that there is always a dubious side to what we had formerly desired. Whatever is unavoidable is decreed to be so by God; it is a part of the universal order of things with its many sublime features, as useful as they are beautiful. Contemplating this fact, we may be elevated to the thought that there are harmonies that we cannot understand in the order of things. The invisible harmonies, Heraclitus dared to say, are even more beautiful than those that are visible.

To be able to accept these thoughts with all that they imply is to achieve a saintly resignation—a source of consolation grounded upon truth—which is incomparably superior to the self-deception in which less elevated souls may put their trust. Such total acceptance is patient resignation in the highest sense of the term.

## IX. Loving and Hating
### (Dictation, May 19, 1907)

*1.* The phenomena of inner perception show us to be substances having psychical accidents.[1] Examples of psychical accidents are:

[1] [Brentano's theory concerning the relation between a substance and its accidents is presented in detail in his *Kategorienlehre* (Leipzig: Felix Meiner, 1933), ed. Alfred Kastil. The following quotation from that work may help to indicate how the term "accident" should be interpreted in the present selection. "Suppose an atom were able to think. Then the thinking atom would be a *whole* of the following sort: once it ceased to think, it would be reduced to one of its parts. The thinking thing could not be said to be capable of surviving the destruction of the atom. This thinking thing as a thinking thing would *include* the atom, in the way in which the concept of something red as such includes the concept of colour. If there were another atom which also thought, then the second atom would also be a second thinking thing, for the thinking thing as a thinking thing would be individuated through the individuality of the atom. We could say that one of the parts is a substance, or substratum, of the whole. The whole may be called an *accident* of the substance. (But it would be a mistake to say that there is a *part* which is an accident of the substance. We are not here dealing with a part that can be separated from the substance or that can be thought about independently of the substance. What we have here are, first, a substance and, secondly, a whole which, as an accident, extends or enriches the substance.)" (P. 152) In answer to the

seeing, hearing, conceptual thinking of various kinds, judging, emotional activity, desiring, pleasure, anger, *etc.* Descartes grouped these together as being "thinking" in the broadest sense of the term. They are uniquely characterized by the fact that they have an object, upon which, as we might say, they are directed. Whoever thinks, thinks about something, whoever is angry is angry about something, and so on. The property of psychical accidents distinguishes every object of inner perception from any object of so-called outer perception.

*2* The objects of inner perception appear non-spatially, and this, too, serves to distinguish them from the objects of outer perception.

*3* Perhaps it may be added that objects of inner perception are further distinguished by the fact that they never appear to us without accidents, while so-called outer perception shows only substantial differences. These latter, contrary to common belief, comprise qualitative determinations, as well as spatial determinations, and thus also size, shape, unity, number (provided these are marks of outer perception, which has been disputed).

*4* It follows that we never perceive our own substance in itself; but it is included in every object of inner perception. Do

---

question, "What is to be counted as a thing or an entity in the strict sense of the term?", Brentano writes: "Not only every substance, and every multiplicity of substances and every part of every substance, but also every accident. The latter contains its substance as part, but not by adding any new part to it. . . . The substratum or substance is not entirely the same as the thing of which it is a substratum. But we must not say that the thing containing the substratum is strictly a *second* thing; for if it were a second thing, it could not contain the first as part." (Pp. 11–12) "One may not say that the substance and the accident together are a multiplicity of things, but only that the substance is a thing and that the substance extended or enriched by means of the accident is a thing, though not a wholly different thing from the substance; hence we do not have here an addition of one thing to another leading to a multiplicity." (P. 54) Brentano notes that, analogously, although an apple is a thing and each of its halves is a thing, they do not together comprise three things. R.M.C.].

we perceive it in its individuality? It is commonly said that we do, but this is not entirely correct.

(a) There are certain determinations of substance which change with every moment (otherwise no distinction with respect to duration would be possible), and we do not perceive these determinations.[2]

(b) We become a primary object of our own thinking when we remember having previously been a secondary object of our own evident inner perception.[3] Then we are able to see clearly that there is a multiplicity of things which *could* correspond to the object of our thought. This accords with the fact that we may think of other souls and of other mental activities, not merely in analogy with ourselves, but exactly in the way in which we think of ourselves. But it is impossible for these other souls to be individually one with ourselves. We think of them only in general terms, and therefore it is obvious that we also think of ourselves only in general terms.

*5* In perceiving ourselves, however, we are aware of perceiving just *one* thing that must be distinguished from every other thing. The justification for this remark is the fact that (1) every positive judgement is particular and (2) no evident apprehension is possible unless that which is apprehending is identical in substance with that which is apprehended.[4] But a multiplicity of substances cannot be identical with each other. The fact that the apprehension is evident thus requires that the object be one substance and not that there be several. Even if there were other objects just like it (so far as *appearances* are concerned), our apprehension presents us with only *one* of them.

---

[2] [Editor's note: Temporal change is a change in substances, but we do not perceive these absolute temporal variations. See Brentano's *Vom sinnlichen und noetischen Bewusstein*, pp. 82–5, 99–123.]

[3] [In every conscious act, according to Brentano, one is aware of onself—at least "*nebenbei*", as a secondary object. Thus if I hear a sound, the sound is the "primary object" of my awareness and I am its secondary object. But if later I recall my hearing the sound, then I become primary object of the later awareness. See *Vom sinnlichen und noetischen Bewusstsein*, p. 77ff. R.M.C.].

[4] [Editor's note: See *Vom sinnlichen und noetischen Bewusstsein*, pp. 1–11.]

*6* This one substance, which is the object of our inner perception, forms a real unity with the accidents that we perceive.

*7* Of these accidents, however, a part may fall away while the others remain, or new accidents may be added to those that are already there. Of the accidents that are given along with the substance in our immediate experience any one may change while the substance as such is unaffected by the change. Indeed all such accidents may fall away simultaneously without any alteration in the substance itself. Possibly this happens during a dreamless sleep or when we have completely lost consciousness.

*8* There can be no accidents in the soul unless the soul is thinking, with its thought directed upon several objects, of which one is the soul itself. But the act which is an accident of the soul cannot be identified merely with objective reference, or direction upon an object. There may be a multiple reference or direction upon an object, incapable of being broken up into simple acts of reference, which comes into being and passes away only *as* a whole; this multiple reference is to be regarded as a *single* real accident. Hence the problem of distinguishing kinds of accidents is not the same as that of distinguishing the ways in which an object may be referred to.

*9* We may distinguish three basic types of reference to an object: (1) thinking, or having the object before the mind; (2) judging; and (3) loving or hating. Thinking may be ranked first, as being the basic and most general type of reference. We cannot form judgements about a thing—we cannot affirm or deny—unless we think about the thing. And we cannot feel love or hate toward a thing unless we think about the thing. Which are we to rank second—judging, or loving and hating? Here the answer may seem less clear. On the one hand, we can love a thing or desire it, without having made any judgement as to whether or not the thing exists. And on the other hand, we can judge about a thing—we can accept or reject it—without loving it or hating it, without desiring or detesting it. Some would rank judging second—after thinking and before the emotions—on the ground that judging is more like thinking than are the emotions. But actually there does not seem to be this greater similarity. Some

LOVING AND HATING

would rank the emotions before judging, and would defend themselves by saying that the will determines whether we believe or do not believe. In general, however, this is not the case. Willing requires judging; and evident inner perception is certainly knowledge which is independent of any willing.

The following points would seem to be the ones that are significant in deciding how to order these phenomena:

(1) Judging accompanies every act of inner perception; but it is possible to conceive of an act of inner perception which is not accompanied by any emotion.

(2) The emotions carry with them a much greater degree of complexity and diversity than does judging.

(3) Just as judging as such adds to the perfection of mere thinking, the emotions in turn appear to contribute a still greater degree of perfection, particularly by means of the feeling of happiness.

These three considerations warrant our saying that judging is the second of the three basic types of objective reference and loving and hating the third.

*10* Let us turn, then, to the subspecies of this third type of reference. It is clear, first of all, that any differences in the thoughts or ideas which underlie our emotions will be carried over into the emotions themselves. This is similar to the way in which substances serve to differentiate their accidents. One's seeing of Peter must be distinct from one's seeing of Paul even though the two seeings are otherwise the same. Similarly, the ways in which a substance changes in the course of time affects its accidents.

Ideas themselves may be distinguished from several different points of view. (1) They may be distinguished by their objects. (2) And (what is connected in a certain way with the first point) they may be distinguished according to whether their objects are thought of in their individuality or only in general terms, and whether they are thought of absolutely or only relatively. (3) Ideas may be distinguished by reference to the temporal mode in which the object is thought. (4) They may be distinguished according to whether the object is thought of positively or negatively. Even if we cannot think of an object negatively without at the same time thinking of it positively, the fact remains that

141

we have here two different relations which are two different ways of referring to an object. As we have already noted, the unity of the act is not at all the same as the unity of the reference to the object. (5) We may distinguish between simple and compound ideas. Compound ideas, in turn, may have a greater or lesser degree of complication; for we can combine attributes in our thinking. Predication may be a matter of judging, as when we say "A tree is green"; but it may also be a matter just of thinking, or having ideas, as when we say "a green tree". And when we form the idea of numbers, such as 2, 3, 5, we compound ideas. We also think in a complex way when we distinguish the parts of a complex object and are able to say that we then have a clearer idea of the whole.[5]

Each of these distinctions, so significant for the sphere of ideas, must correspond to a distinction within the sphere of *love and hate*.

(1) First of all, love, and also hate, may be distinguished according to its object.

(2) They may also be distinguished according to whether they are general or are directed upon some concrete particular, and so on.

(3) They may be distinguished according to the temporal mode with respect to which the object is loved or hated. In this way, we distinguish the *regret* which pertains to the past, the *pain* or *sorrow* which is directed upon a present experience, and the *fear* of an evil to come.

(4) The emotional relations may be distinguished as positive or negative; it is this distinction which finds expression in the terms "love" and "hate".

(5) The distinction between simple and compound ideas, and of the ways of compounding ideas, should also have bearing upon the ways in which the emotions are directed upon their objects.

*11* Distinctions with respect to judgement, like those with respect to ideas, carry over into the sphere of the emotions. Thus my emotion will differ markedly depending upon whether

[5] [Editor's note: According to Brentano's later view, the second and fourth points are untenable, since we think only in general terms and have no negative ideas. He had also held prior to the time of this dictation (1907) that we have no negative ideas.]

some future happiness, which I may picture for myself, appears certain or uncertain, probable or improbable, attainable or unattainable. Again there may be something which is in itself indifferent to me, but which pleases me as being a *sign* of some other thing, or as being *instrumental* to some other thing; such an emotion is quite obviously influenced by judging. Indeed the simplest pleasures of the senses are characterized by the fact that they are experiences which we love and which we apprehend with evidence. We see the same thing in connection with willing and intending or undertaking. No one can will a thing he believes to be beyond his power, however much he may desire it. And no one can form the intention of doing something if he believes that he will never have the opportunity to do it. In such cases, the essential nature of the reference of our emotions is affected by the particular characteristics of the judgements underlying them. The nature of these emotions may perhaps be compared with the particular characteristics of the evident, in virtue of which we are able to distinguish judgements which are evident from judgements which are blind.

12 There are other distinctions which hold exclusively within the sphere of the emotions.

One is the distinction between *loving*, simply, and *preferring*. The latter act involves comparison. If I prefer one thing to another, then I love the one thing more and the other less. Similarly for hating; if I hate one thing more than another, then the one thing could be called, if the expression were permitted, the "preferred object of hate", and the other thing "the less preferred object of hate". In the sphere of judging, there is a true and a false, but of things that are true none of them is *more* true than another, and nothing is *held* to be more true than anything else.

12a Suppose a person loves something that is inseparably bound up with something that he hates. In such a case, he might prefer that neither exist and thus sacrifice what he loves. Or he might prefer that both exist, thus taking what he hates as part of the bargain. We could say, in the first case, that he hates the one thing more than he loves the other; and we could say, in the second case, that he loves the one thing more than he hates the other. In the first case, in which the love wins out, we could also say that the thing that is hated in and for itself is loved implicitly as an inseparable part of the whole. And in the second case, in which the hate wins out, we could say that the thing is loved in and for itself is implicitly hated as an inseparable part of the whole.

*13* Moreover, there is, in the sphere of the emotions, a *correct* loving or hating and an *incorrect* loving or hating. This may seem to be the analogue of correct acceptance or affirmation and correct rejection or denial, but it is essentially different.

*14* And there is that which is loved or hated in itself, or for its own sake, and that which is loved or hated for the sake of something else. In the latter case, we have the useful and the harmful. One might wish to compare this distinction with the distinction between judgements which affirm or deny something *directly*, and judgements which affirm or deny something *indirectly* [i.e., as a result of inference]. But the comparison fails in essential respects: what we infer we also hold to be true in itself, but what we love for the sake of something else may be something we do not hold to be good in itself.

*14a* The useful is loved for the sake of some other thing; so, too, for whatever is a *sign* of what is good. One might wish to say the sign is also an instance of the useful, since a sign is a *means* to our apprehension of what is good and this apprehension is itself loved and appears to us as a good. But we are concerned here, not with the goodness of the apprehension as such, but with the good which is apprehended. In the same way a sign of what is bad is unloved, despite the fact that in being instrumental to knowledge it is instrumental to something that is good. If the sign is to be counted as useful, it is only as a means to the joy or pleasure which knowledge gives.

In much the way that we love the useful, we love the inseparable constituents of the things we love, even though some of these constituents may be such that we would hate them if we were to consider them in and for themselves. Or consider an example of the reverse situation. A man may wish to attend both the opera and the theatre; but being able to do only one of these things, he decides to attend the theatre and not the opera. In such a case the opera is loved in and for itself and hated only implicitly, as being something which stands in the way of the alternative enjoyment. The martyr who finds he cannot persevere in his faith unless he suffers pain chooses to suffer. He hates the pain in and for itself, but he loves it implicitly as a means to his perseverance. A whole cannot exist without its parts. But a whole may be loved as a whole and yet contain parts which are themselves not loved but hated as wholes. The parts, however, are loved implicitly, just as the means to what is good are loved implicitly. But such parts do not make the whole a greater good in the way in which they would if they were loved in and for themselves.

*15* There is another analogy between the emotions and judgement—but it is only an analogy. Sometimes we have an insight into the correctness of love or hate (either simple love or hate or preference) and sometimes we do not. If we have an indirect insight into such correctness, then this presupposes some other direct insight. The logical connection is to be understood in accordance with the usual rules of judgement. When we do have a direct insight into the correctness of an emotion, then the emotion is experienced as being correct. Sometimes, but by no means always, we have such an insight when we love or hate something in itself.

*16* But there have been opposing errors with respect to this point.

Some would say that *everything* a person loves in itself is something which for him is good and worthy of love, and that *everything* he hates in itself is something which for him is bad and worthy of hate. And they would make a similar claim regarding preference. According to this view, whenever anything is loved in itself, this love is experienced as being correct.

There are others who would say that there is *nothing* in virtue of which such love or hate can be called correct. On this second view, one might nevertheless speak of a correct or incorrect endeavour—correct if one pursues a greater interest at the expense of a lesser, and incorrect if one pursues a lesser interest at the expense of a greater. The one striving or endeavour might be called praiseworthy and the other blameworthy, but praise and blame, on this view, would have no place in connection with any direct interest in an object as such.

If we look at the matter properly, we can see that in the end the first of these two views comes ultimately to the same thing as the second. Whoever affirms that correctness is only subjective thereby falsifies the concept of correctness. It is as though one were to speak of a purely subjective truth. For Protagoras, there is no possibility of anything being false. We should not be surprised that the first of these two views is essentially the same as that of Protagoras: so far as our love or hate pertains to that which is to be loved or to be hated in and for itself, there is no possibility of incorrectness. Everything is simply a matter of taste.

*16a* This error is profound and extensive; it has consequences which would undermine any exalted way of looking at the world. If all good were subjective, then there could be no concept of God as constituting the highest good. The highest good for one person would not be the highest good for another.

*17* Experience shows that, when we love, or hate, something in itself, this love or hate is in some instances experienced as being correct, and in other instances not. This is similar to what we find in the sphere of judgement, where some direct judgements are themselves evident and others not. Instinctive drives, such as hunger and thirst, and the greed that one's habits are likely to produce, are not experienced as correct. But we *are* able to see that we love correctly when we love knowledge, joy, correct love itself, justice, thinking, and the like. And we are also able to see that our *preference* is correct when, other things being equal, we prefer knowing to not knowing, or knowing more to knowing less, and when we prefer that many, rather than few, be happy, or that they be happy rather than unhappy. If someone were to say that in such cases a contrary preference would make no difference and that we are concerned here only with matters of taste, we would immediately recognize his assertion as absurd.

*18* Closer study of these instances of correct emotion shows that they are not only similar to directly evident judgements in general; they bear a specific resemblance to those directly evident judgements in which the truth of the judgement is clear from the *concepts* which the judgement involves. Such judgements are made when contemplation of the object causes an evident rejection or denial, a rejection or denial that is seen to be correct. Thus if we attempt to imagine a round square, we are forced to deny or reject it, for we see that it is impossible. In much the same way, contemplation of knowledge causes a love that is experienced as being correct and contemplation of a painful experience—this being an experience which hates itself, so to speak—causes a feeling of hatred that is experienced as being correct. Consequently our knowledge of the correctness of such love or hatred is *apodictic*; we know that *only* love or hatred can be correct in these cases. Such love and hatred is similar to the apodictic judgement. For apodictic judgements, like these emotions, arise out of the contemplation of their objects.

*19* It is easy to see how one might arrive at a different view about the way in which we come to know that certain things are to be loved in and for themselves. One might be tempted to think that we perceive a kind of congruence, such as the congruence that holds between two triangles, but that this congruence holds between the concept of the object, on the one hand, and the love that is experienced as correct, on the other. Thus it might be held that when we contemplate knowledge, there arises out of this contemplation a correct love of knowledge; this correct love and the knowledge are then intertwined in our intuition, so to speak; and they fit together in such a way that the concept of being worthy of love is to be found in the concept of knowledge. Actually, however, although love may arise out of contemplation of knowledge, the concept of being worthy of love is certainly not to be found in the concept of knowledge. The kind of congruence that holds between triangles is not present here. We can speak of congruence only in an entirely different sense, meaning simply the *correctness* of the love that is involved. To choose between this view and the one that I have proposed, we would have to answer the following question. If the love, instead of arising from the concept of knowledge, were somehow intertwined with the knowledge, as knowledge itself can become entertwined with pain, error, and doubt, could we have our apodictic awareness that knowledge is worthy of love? Would the concept of a knowledge that is *not* worthy of love still contain something like a contradiction? It seems to me the question is easy to answer. Let us assume that the concept of correct love, as distinguished from the simpler concept of love, has somehow been drawn from our experience. This could only happen in the way that I have described: from the concept of the object there arises a love of that object, and the love is experienced as being correct. If what I have said is right, then we need not look elsewhere for the concept of correct love. But if it is not right and we bring in the concept of correctness from elsewhere, then we will have no criterion for applying this concept and we will be unable to see, for example, that the love of knowledge is something that is necessarily correct. Surely no one would hold that the concept of being loved correctly, or of being correct to love, is contained in the knowledge itself.

20 The concepts of good and bad, and of pleasure and displeasure, require further clarification.

In the *Nichomachaean Ethics*, Aristotle draws a distinction, not only between what is good and what is agreeable, but also between what is good *simply* and by nature and what is good *for someone* or incidentally, as well as between what is *agreeable* in itself and what is agreeable for someone or incidentally.

The agreeable is that in which we take pleasure; it is what we find pleasurable. The connections between pleasure and certain activities have been arranged purposively by nature, as have the organs of the body. But just as unhealthy malformations may develop in the organs of the body, pleasure may occasionally become attached to abnormal objects. If pleasure is to be normal in the life of the adult, he should have a normal life during the period of growth and education (whether the education be a matter of natural experience or of care and guidance). If the earlier life has not been normal, one should try to change one's habits in such a way that the normal connection with pleasure will be restored. Thus what is agreeable, or more agreeable, *by nature* must be distinguished from that which is agreeable, or more agreeable, *incidentally*, for some particular individual. Abnormal pleasures can never be as rich or as complete as those that are normal. Consider the following analogy: if a pianist acquires the habit of fingering a certain passage in an improper way, he may find it easier to continue to play it in that way, but he will never find it as easy as he would have, had he begun by playing it properly.

So much, then, for the distinction between what is agreeable in itself and what is agreeable incidentally, where both cases involve blind, instinctive love and pleasure.

And how are we to construe the Aristotelian distinction between what is *good simply* and what is *good for someone*? The distinction applies, not to those things that are good in the sense of being useful, but to those that are good in themselves. It might be thought that Aristotle has the following sort of thing in mind. We may distinguish between realizing what is good in general, a good in the whole world-order, and realizing a good in a particular individual. If at the Last Judgement a greater amount of bliss were given to a person who actually deserved it less, then he would have a greater amount of good than he otherwise would have, but the good in the universe, considered as a whole, would be less. But I do not believe that this is the distinction Aristotle had in mind. I think he was concerned instead with this type of situation. Consider a man whose preferences are abnormal. Of two things, A and B, such that A is the one that is to be preferred, he nevertheless incorrectly prefers B. The man would feel more satisfaction if B were realized than he would if A were realized. If B *is* realized, then the feeling of satisfaction he would have is a good. And he would not have *this* good, if A, the object of correct preference, had been realized. But to have this greater degree of satisfaction in the correct case instead of in the incorrect case would be a greater good in and for itself. For the man of abnormal dispositions, the relations among goods are distorted.

Aristotle does not apply the word "good" merely to that which is loved or to that which is capable of being loved; he reserves it for what is *correctly* loved, or capable of being *correctly* loved. Here, then, we have what he called "good simply".

We should not, therefore, attempt to distinguish between those acts which are correct for an erring conscience and those acts which are correct for me. And if we are considering a man who is not yet fully developed with respect to virtue, we should not attempt to distinguish between those acts which are better or more advisable for him and those acts which are worthy of being recommended in themselves.

*21* Some things are incompatible with others. A physical thing cannot be both round and square at one and the same time, or in motion and at rest, or liquid and solid, or red and blue. If someone *desires*, or *wills*, or *wants* that an object be one of these things, then he cannot at the same time reasonably desire, will, or want that it be the other. But one can *look favourably upon* the object being one of these things and at the same time also look favourably upon its being the other: one can look favourably upon the object being round and one can also look favourably upon the object being square, and so on. The love that is involved in this second type of case is quite different from that which is involved in desiring, wanting, or willing. How are we to describe the distinction?

Should we say that in the second case the love that is involved is directed merely upon the *idea* of the thing and not upon the thing? This does not seem to be the correct answer. Consider the case where the objects of thought happen to be certain high-minded endeavours, of the sort that we might find in art, science, or politics, but endeavours that are incompatible with each other. Surely it is the endeavours themselves that we can be said to look upon favourably or to love. Should we say, then, that what we love or favour are indeed the various incompatible endeavours, but that the object of our love or favour is not that there *be* such endeavours? We would thus have a way of contrasting this love or favour with desiring, wanting, and willing. Desiring, wanting, and willing are directed toward the *being* of things: We want or will *that* the things exist.

Or should we say that the object of such love or favour is *that* there be such things—and then add that, since the thing loved is incompatible with a certain other good, the love is inseparably bound up with hatred, with the hatred against there being such things (or, what comes to the same thing, with the love of there *not* being such things)? Wanting and willing could then be said to be a matter of preferring the being of an object to its non-being. I look favourably upon one of the two incompatible pursuits and I *also* look favourably upon the other; yet I may *prefer* one of them to the other. The love of the one and the love of the other thus function as two opposing weights in a scale; at most one can tip the scale. Or they may counter-balance each other: if the agent is then to want or desire one thing rather than the other, or, in the case where he can bring about the things himself, if he is then to will one thing rather than the other, some further motive must be added to tip the scale. In such a case, one may say, "I *wish* that the one thing were compatible with the other." But it would be absurd to say, "I *want* the one thing to be compatible with the other".

How then are we to draw the distinction between love of the more simple sort and desiring, wanting, and willing? The question involves the distinction already discussed between loving, simply, and preferring. To prefer, however, is not *ipso facto* to want, will, or desire. Suppose there are three mutually incompatible goods, A, B, and C; I might prefer B to A, but also prefer C to B, with the result that B, though preferred to A, is no more wanted, willed, or desired than is A. We must say, therefore, that in order to become an object of will, want, or desire, the thing that is loved must be preferred, not only to some one thing that is incompatible with it, but also to every possible object that is thought to be incompatible with it. But the simpler type of love, which does not thus involve wanting, willing, or desiring, is directed upon things considered in abstraction from the actual circumstances in which they occur. And similarly for the simpler form of preference. But wanting, willing, and desiring do not thus abstract from circumstances; they involve a preference that takes into account whatever I happen to be aware of at that particular moment. It should be noted that I can thus want or desire a thing without at all believing it to be something I can bring about myself. I can want or desire that the weather be good tomorrow, but I have no *choice* in the matter.

22 What *is* the distinctive nature of choosing? Does choosing consist simply in the desire that a certain thing happen coupled with an awareness of the fact that the realization of the thing depends upon me? Must I not also believe that the object of my desire or preference will be realized in *consequence* of my desire or preference? To be sure, the thing need not be a direct consequence of my desire or preference, as it is, say, when I will to move my hand and thereby move it. It might be an indirect

consequence, as when I issue a command, or when I resolve to do something at some later date, thus commanding myself, so to speak, to perform a certain action in the future. In this latter case, I can properly be said to set myself to do something later; I set myself for a subsequent act of will, where the act of will is the sort performed in other cases to bring about directly the act in question.

By appeal to these distinctions, we are able to throw light upon some of the more important respects in which the various emotions may differ from each other.

*23* There is a certain kind of willing and choosing (also, strictly speaking, of wanting and desiring) which presents a distinctive complication. I can want either this or that to happen in order only that some third thing might thereby be prevented. I can also desire that, if of two cases A and B, case A should occur then something else C should also occur, and that if case B should occur then C should not occur. These various provisions and stipulations set limits to my desires. Willing and choosing are essentially similar. Consider a chess move made at an advanced stage of the game. In making the move, I have already decided, in a certain way, what my subsequent moves will be; I have taken into consideration the many different ways in which my opponent might counter the move and I have then decided, for each case, what my own next move will be. It is only by doing this that one is able to announce, as chess masters sometimes do, that one's opponent will be mated within so many moves. I am not the one who makes all of the moves, and it is not within my power to make my opponent's decisions for him. But my complex act of will—my complex decision—has taken hypothetical account of every case that could conceivably arise.

*24* What are we to say of such emotions as fear, hope, dread, anxiety, agitation, jealousy, envy, anger, terror, horror, uneasiness, lust, disgust—and so on and so forth? In almost every one of these cases we are dealing with an extraordinarily complex phenomenon. Many of the terms are difficult to define; we cannot fix their range of application with any degree of exactness. We come to learn them, not by means of definitions, but by using them in a variety of actual situations. Compare the concept of a high mountain. No one is able to define it so precisely that he could say, of a mountain that was not high, that it *would* be high if only one foot were added. The question of what it is for one person to be angry is similar. Can one be angry with a non-living thing, such as a chair? Can one be angry with a man who lived many centuries in the past? Or can one be angry with someone who is depicted on the stage or in a novel? If one *can* be angry in these cases, must one have forgotten, for the moment, that the chair is not a living thing, that the historical person belongs to the distant past, and that the person depicted by the poet is only a thing of the imagination? Such questions readily lead to disputes that are merely verbal.

But a scientific treatment could accomplish this much: (a) it could contribute toward the analysis of particular, individual phenomena; (b) by appeal to philogy, it could set more or less definite limits to the use of certain ordinary expressions; and (c), what is of most importance for psychology, it could tell us what particular emotive phenomena, and what groups of such phenomena, are related genetically to each other. Since genetic laws are not exact, we would have to take into account the probability of various connections and relations. Psychological phenomena are connected genetically with physical phenomena, as well as with other psychological phenomena, and these connections can be indicated with some degree of probability for the complex cases we have mentioned. Thus it frequently happens that a frightened man becomes pale and trembles, whereas an angry man becomes both warm and red, "glowing" with anger. There may well be considerable doubt, therefore, about what essential mark of this class of cases really is.

Let us consider the angry man in more detail. It would seem that he wants to inflict evil upon a person toward whom he is hostile, a person who has interfered in some way with some of his own interests. But we cannot call him angry in virtue of this characteristic alone. He must also feel agitated and be seething with a rage which, like a kind of madness, is capable of overpowering him and carrying him away. He clenches his fist against the enemy, even though the enemy may be off in the distance entirely out of reach, and he grinds his teeth, as though he could tear the enemy into bits and then grind him into powder. Above all, the motive for his anger may disappear entirely from his memory, just as the danger to himself may go entirely unheeded; his wild excitement will continue to strengthen his hostile urge to inflict harm.

We know, of course, that animals are also capable of anger. The dog, for example, is easily made angry, because of his instincts, and his anger will quickly rise to a level of great vehemence. Anger in dogs is very much like fear in sheep; as soon as the sheep sees a. wolf, he is instinctively overcome with fear. Similarly, other animals may be overcome by hunger, or by thirst, or during mating season by the sexual urge. The essential characteristic of the angry man is the overpowering urge to inflict harm, an urge which may have no clear motive and which is bound up with a great variety of passions and reflexes.

If one were able to excite all of these side-effects in a dog, then probably one could also create in him the urge to do harm, without his knowing what it is that he wishes to harm. Aristotle pointed out, similarly, that since fear makes one cold, people are often made fearful merely by becoming cold, without knowing what it is that they fear. If, therefore, the desire to inflict harm can induce a state of agitation and excitement, while, on the other hand, the state of agitation and excitement can create the desire to inflict harm, we may wonder whether the first or the second of these marks constitutes the essence of anger. We may do well in the meantime to regard the essence of anger as comprising, not only both of these things, but also a genetic relation to some prior experience which occasioned the whole hostile state. In the case of man, anger is commonly bound up with a desire for vengeance—a vengeance which is not merely a matter of receiving a just and proper compensation. The angry man would take out his vengeance on the enemy himself; he would cool off his anger by inflicting harm upon his enemy.

25 There are two senses in which a man may be said to be pleased with an object or to take pleasure in it, and two senses in which he may be said to be displeased with an object or to take displeasure in it. In the first case, he may simply find the object to be agreeable, or disagreeable. In the second, he finds the object to be agreeable, or disagreeable, and then, because of this fact, he takes pleasure or displeasure in *another* object. As a result of his

being pleased, or displeased, with the first object, there redounds a *sensuous* pleasure or displeasure.

One sometimes uses the expression "intensive" in connection with intellectual or spiritual pleasures and displeasures. But this is proper only when sensuous pleasure or displeasure thus redounds from these higher activities; for what is intensive must be such that it is either itself continuous and extended in space or an object that is continuous and extended in space.[6] When Newton read that his astronomical hypotheses had been confirmed by new measurements, his joy became more and more intense and he was finally so overcome that he could no longer continue reading. He succumbed to the intensive sensuous pleasure which had redounded from his higher feelings. The same was true of Archimedes when he called out "Eureka!" as though intoxicated. Even those pleasures one may take in the awareness of virtue or vice may give rise to violent sensuous passions.

Thus Aristotle proposed, in the final book of the *Nicomachaean Ethics*, that the feelings of pleasure accompanying our intellectual activities belong to them naturally, even though they are not an intrinsic part of those activities. But he never sufficiently investigated the problem of intensities, and did not go into further detail.

*26* This redounding of sensuous pleasure and displeasure is striking on its own, and also because of a further circumstance. When sensuous pleasure or displeasure thus redounds from our being pleased or displeased with something, the object of the sensuous pleasure or displeasure is not the same as the first object with which we are pleased or displeased. Mill noted that sensuous pleasures and displeasures may be distinguished according to

[6] [Sensuous pleasure and displeasure, according to Brentano, have as their primary objects acts of sensation (and these latter are a subspecies of the first of the three basic types of psychological phenomena); acts of sensation have as *their* objects various sense-qualities, such as colours, sounds, tastes; these sense-qualities according to Brentano, are physical and not psychological; and sensuous pleasure and displeasure (which are subspecies of loving and hating, the third basic type of psychological phenomenon) are not sense-qualities, but are psychological and therefore intentional phenomena. See Brentano's *Untersuchungen zur Sinnespsychologie*, pp. 119–25, and his *Vom sinnlichen und noetischen Bewusstsein*, pp. 16–18, 80–1, 138–9. R.M.C.].

quality as well as according to quantity. The quantitative[7] characteristics are exhibited in the sensuous qualities of the objects of such pleasure and displeasure, but these pleasures and displeasures take on a higher quality because of their association with the higher activities from which they redound. Aristotle said that the pleasure that is thus associated with noble actions is the only pleasure that is good, the pleasure that is associated with actions that are bad is the only pleasure that is bad; other pleasures he views as neither good nor bad. But he also had a somewhat different thought in this connection. It was what Fechner expressed, more recently, in saying that every sensuous pleasure, regarded in and for itself, is good, and that such pleasure can be said to be bad only to the extent that it is aroused by one's being pleased with what is detestable.

*26a* Aristotle thought that the connection between these two types of pleasure was so intimate that, if the awareness of a certain truth gives us sensuous pleasure, then we should experience the pleasure every time we contemplate that truth; if we do not, he said, it is because our powers of concentration are not sufficiently strong and the knowledge or awareness forsakes us. But this assertion is disconfirmed by our experience of pleasure and displeasure on hearing music, where repetition influences us now more, now less, and may even cause our pleasure to turn into pain. What fails us when we thus cease to feel pleasure would seem to be, not our powers of concentration or our knowledge and awareness, but our capacity for experiencing the sensuous pleasure that may accompany this knowledge or awareness. (It is not that our degree of attentiveness diminishes or that our awareness becomes less perfect, for the repeated experience makes the awareness easier to attain.) What makes an enormous difference, so far as the phenomenon of redundancy is concerned, is the consciousness of making a discovery and of progressing, as well as the various other mental activities that contribute to this consciousness.

*27* This redounding, the fact that sensuous pleasure and displeasure are aroused as side-effects of certain activities, resembles

[7] [Translators' note: Reading *"quantitativen"* in place of *"qualitativen"*.]

our various instincts in exhibiting an extraordinary teleological feature of our physical life.

*28* A correct *love* that arises out of concepts manifests itself as being necessarily correct, and the same holds for correct *preference*. In the former case, we arrive at a knowledge of what is *good*; in the latter case, we arrive at a knowledge of what is *better*.

*29* It cannot be claimed that each time we think of a good thing, a love of that thing must arise out of the concept. But it is certain that when a love *does* arise out of the concept, then the correctness of the love may be known with certainty, and the thing loved is *known directly* to be good. And similarly for preference: it need not always arise out of the concepts of the things concerned, but whenever it does, then we know that the preferred thing is the better one.

*30* There are a number of different cases in which preference may be experienced as being correct. Thus I may know that a thing is good and prefer its being to its non-being. I may know that a thing is bad and prefer its non-being to its being. There may be two good things just alike and therefore both such that they ought to be loved—even if the one good is to be realized in me and the other in someone else. Without such a principle our theory of value would degenerate into subjectivism. (Pascal, however much of a sceptic he may be otherwise, gives unreserved support to this principle whenever the occasion arises.) Again, a correct preference may arise out of concepts when we are weighing goods against evils; the goods, of course, will be treated as positive quantities and the evils as negative.

Pascal also holds that there are classes of goods which can be ranked in the following way: the smallest of any of the goods that are to be found in the higher class will always be superior to the totality of goods to be found in the lower class. Thus he would say that minds or souls and also, apparently, acts of knowledge are goods such that any one of them is higher than all physical things put together; and an act of holy love is better than *any* amount of knowledge.

There are others who take similar views. Thus Herbart places morality so high that, of all the things that may be said to have value, only morality, he thinks, gives value to the *person*. Curiously enough, he treats knowledge and the other aspects of mental life as though they were mere externals. And he seems to look upon morality as pertaining *only* to character and not to what a person actually does; he would scarcely venture to say that the value of a person at any given moment is determined by what the person happens to be doing at that moment. But this emphasis upon character hardly accords with what Aristotle found to be obvious: that the activity is always superior in value to the disposition. What, he asked, would be worthy of honour or veneration in an intellect that was equipped with all possible knowledge but remained forever inactive, as though it were eternally asleep?

*31* Hume held that a lifeless, physical thing could not be in itself an object of love or hate (or at any rate this seems to be the supposition underlying some of the things he says). But if this were so, and if it were right that it be so, then, as Pascal thought, the number of physical things could be increased to infinity without having as much value as one mind or soul. Perhaps it cannot be contested that an act of saintly or supernatural love, however slight, belongs to a superior class of goods—providing that, as the Church teaches, every such act makes us worthy of contemplating God and leads to such contemplation as its proper reward. The value of such love would simply be a consequence of the perfection of God, which is infinitely superior to everything else.

*32* It is quite possible for there to be a class of goods which could be increased *ad indefinitum* but without exceeding a given finite good. Geometry treats of quantities that are infinitely smaller than other quantities; for any fraction you can think of there will be a quantity smaller than it; and then there will be still other quantities that are infinitely smaller than they are. One could even say that the surface of a table is larger than a stretch of time extending into infinity.

*33* God's decision to create the world was based upon a preference for the best that is possible. We should be sceptical, therefore, toward any scheme of values that is likely to conflict with this fact.

Pascal had spoken of three ranks of value, but quite obviously this number does not exhaust the kinds of goods there are. Next to God, the highest possible good is the created universe itself, though not if it is falsely conceived as existing alone and apart from God. What God loves above all else is himself taken together with the created universe.

It may be that the universe contains some things which, considered in themselves, are bad and other things which are without value. I, too, am inclined to believe that a universe containing *only* physical things would be a vain endeavour. It would be inferior, not only to any single human spirit, but to the soul of a dog with its sensations and passions. Contrast such a soul-less universe with the magnificent way in which the world actually has evolved, with the development of life, sensation, reason, and the highest types of love.

What if there were *no* physical world? Then there would be nothing enabling one mind or soul to come into contact with another. There would be no sensual pleasure and pain, and hence no distribution of such pleasure and pain would be essential to a just arrangement of the world. In such a world, God might possibly inspire isolated acts of love in individual souls. But could that world in any stage of its development be better than or even equal in value to this one? I cannot see that it would, and I say this for reasons other than the feeling that I actually have for the divine decision.

*34* It is clear that, in comparing amounts of value, we cannot arrive at exact measurements. In practice, therefore, there will be an area in which each of us may follow his own inclinations. But even with this freedom, we will have a tremendous task if we are always to give preference to what is known to be better.

For instance, there is an obligation to love one's neighbour. But this is consistent with having a special concern for oneself and for a certain circle of one's intimates, provided and to the extent that this concern contributes to the greatest possible good, particularly within society. What would be the result if each person were to watch over the virtue and personal affairs of his neighbours in the way in which he watches over his own? And so, too, for other matters.

So far as knowledge and virtue are concerned, it is clear that, whatever value they may have in relation to each other, they should be so fostered that they will have the greatest possible use within the sphere that each person can influence. As for pleasure, the wise thing is not to make it an end in itself but to seek it only as a means to other goods. If we cultivate science or seek to live a moral and virtuous life, then there are certain distinctive pleasures that we will enjoy. If we eat and drink out of concern for the preservation of the body and of the human species, then, too, we will have distinctive pleasures which nature, in its wisdom, has arranged. And similarly for countless other cases. But if a chain of calamities has reduced one to a sickly and melancholy state, then the inclination to seek out sensuous pleasure as an aid and remedy against temptation will take on a far greater significance. When St. Francis of Assisi counselled his brothers to "serve the Lord joyfully", he hoped thereby to make it easier for them to follow still another commandment: "*Vinum, ut laetificet cor hominibus.*"

But this remains forever true:

> Folgst du der Lust mit sehender Brust, sie ziehet und fliehet:
> Wählst du zu Edlem die Bahn, folgt sie dir liebend hinan.[8]

Thus Aristotle could say that only the noble man is truly happy. History has shown us again and again, up to the present, that the voluptuary quickly becomes apathetic, viewing the world as Leopardi painted it: a bore, a slough, and a realm of infinite frivolity.

[8] [Translator's note: The sense of Brentano's distich is: If you lust after pleasure it stays out of reach, but it comes on its own if you strive for the best.]

# Introduction to the 1934 Edition

## By Oskar Kraus

---

Franz Brentano's treatise, *Vom Ursprung sittlicher Erkenntnis*, first published in 1889, has had great influence upon modern theory of value. Edmund Husserl embraced its tenets in the *Logische Untersuchungen*, as did Meinong in his address, "Für die Psychologie und gegen den Psychologismus in der allgemeinen Werttheorie."[1] Max Scheler's principal book, *Der Formalismus in der Ethik und die materiale Wertethik*, despite its distortions and superficialities, may be traced to the same source.[2] Nicolai Hartmann's *Ethik*, even with its realm of value, rich with *entia irrealia*, could not have come into being without Brantano's work.[3] Countless other works on ethics and theory of value could also be listed in this context. Reviewing the English translation of the first edition of Brentano's work, the esteemed British philosopher, G. E. Moore, praised Brentano's work in the strongest terms. He said: "This is a far better discussion of the most fundamental principles of Ethics than any others with which I am acquainted. ... In almost all points in which he differs from any of the great historical systems, he is in the right; and he differs with regard to the most

[1] Edmund Husserl, *Logische Untersuchungen* (Halle: Max Niemeyer, 1900–1); Alexius Meinong, "Für die Psychologie und gegen den Psychologismus in der allgemeinen Werttheorie", *Logos*, Vol. III (1912), pp. 1–14.

[2] Max Scheler, *Der Formalismus in der Ethik und die materiale Wertethik* (Halle: Max Niemeyer, 1913–16).

[3] Nicolai Hartmann, *Ethik* (Berlin, 1926); translated by Stanton Coit as *Ethics* (London: Allen & Unwin, 1932), three volumes.

fundamental points of Moral Philosophy. . . . It would be difficult to exaggerate the importance of the work."[4] I would say, indeed, that Brentano's work is the most significant step forward that has been made in ethics and the theory of value since the era of classical Greek philosophy.

The Sophists had sought to undermine the ethical bases of the law and the state. It was Socrates who taught, in opposition to them, that there is such a thing as *knowledge* within the sphere of ethics and that the natural foundations for law and morality are to be found within ourselves. Plato knew and taught, accordingly, that no authority could be the source of morality. It is not because God wills as he does that certain things are right and good; on the contrary, the most perfect being can will only that which is good in itself or that which leads to the good and to the best. Both Plato and Aristotle held that feeling and willing may be correct or incorrect, just as judging and believing may be correct or incorrect. Brentano shows that the standard for the correctness and incorrectness of feeling and willing lies in certain psychological activities, and he shows us what those activities are. Like his great predecessors, he took up the battle against the spirit of Sophistry which, at the present time as well as in antiquity, is represented by the doctrine of the subjectivity and relativity of all knowledge and value.

Within the realm of logic, Protagoras had defended the proposition that what each man believes is true for him and that in consequence man is the measure of all things—of that which is, that it is, and of that which is not, that it is not. Other Sophists were to carry this doctrine over into the realm of ethics, saying that what each man loves is good for him and that what each man hates is bad for him, so that in consequence one and the same thing may be both good in itself and bad in itself—good for all those who love it, and bad for all those who hate it.

Given this point of view, there could be no genuine knowledge and no system of values possessing general validity. The concept of correct judgement or belief would be as untenable and fictitious as that of justified love, evaluation, and endeavour. On such a view, it would be senseless to say of a judgement that it

[4] G. E. Moore, *International Journal of Ethics*, Vol. XIV (1903), pp. 123–8; the quotation is on page 123. Compare Moore's *Principia Ethica* (Cambridge: the University Press, 1903), pp. x–xi.

is simply correct, or that its contradictory is incorrect, and therefore it would also be senseless to say that there are judgements which may serve as guidelines for the formation of other judgements. And it would be senseless to say of any interest or pleasure that it is itself simply justified, and therefore there would be nothing to which we could oppose unjustified interest, desire, or pleasure. Hence logic and ethics as normative disciplines would be impossible.

But a sophisticated psychology can uproot the logical subjectivism of Protagoras. An adequate theory of knowledge would exhibit the *evident judgement* as the ultimate standard for determining what is correct or incorrect within the sphere of judgement. Leibniz distinguished two principal types of immediately certain truth. There are, first, the "truths of fact"—those immediately certain perceptions by means of which we are able to apprehend our own present states of mind without any possibility of error. Thus we are immediately aware of ourselves at the present moment as thinking and judging and feeling. And there are, secondly, the "truths of reason"—those axiomatic, *a priori* insights by means of which we are able to reject apodictically the objects of certain combinations of concepts, in other words, to reject them as impossible. Thus if a man has a round square as the object of his thought, he will recognize immediately that such an object cannot exist. Evident judgements of these two types constitute the norm or standard for all other judgements. For it is only on the basis of such judgements as these that we can form the concept of what it is for a judgement to be *correct*. A judgement may be said to be correct, or true, if no evident judgement about the same object could contradict it. The evident judgement is the logical standard or norm of correctness.[5]

In the investigations that follow, Brentano shows that the

[5] Compare Brentano's *Wahrheit und Evidenz* (Leipzig: Felix Meiner, 1930), ed. Oskar Kraus; translated as *The True and the Evident* (London: Routledge and Kegan Paul, 1966), English edition edited by Roderick M. Chisholm. "Truth pertains to the judgement of the person who judges correctly—to the judgement of the person who judges about a thing in the way in which anyone whose judgements were *evident* would judge about the thing; hence it pertains to the judgement of one who asserts what the person whose judgements were evident would also assert." English edition, p. 122; German edition, p. 139.

concept of the evident has its analogue in ethics. In ethics, too, there is a standard of correctness. Our consciousness is such that we can speak meaningfully of correct feeling, correct preferring, and correct willing. There are norms that entail obligations; there is right and justice; and there are things that are good or valuable in themselves. Brentano does not present us with a system of ethics in the present work, though he presented such a system in his lectures on ethics.[6] Rather, he analyzes the ethical consciousness which is active in all of us. He follows this analysis to those ultimate experiences from which we derive the concept of *correctness*, as applied to feelings, evaluations, and preferences. These experiences are of emotions that are justified in themselves, and from them we derive our *a priori* axioms of value and of preference.

This book, as Brentano himself observed, is concerned with descriptive psychology; it is here that its principal value lies.

One must not suppose that those acts of evaluation and preference that are experienced as being correct provide us with practical norms which set up one and the same goal for all creatures to strive at. One must distinguish the concepts of *value* and *good* from those of *practical goal* and *practical good*. The latter can be different for each person, even though the former are the same for all.

"Good in itself" is analogous to "exists". A thing may be said to *exist* if it is such that any evident judgement having it as object must be affirmative. A thing is *good in itself* if it is such that any emotion experienced as being correct and having it as object must be positive and not negative—love rather than hate. Analogously for what is bad in itself, or evil. As we have said, a judgement is correct if it is impossible for an evident judgement having the same object to be of the contrary quality. Analogously, an emotion is correct if it is impossible for an emotion having the same object and itself experienced as being correct to have the contrary quality.

We see, therefore, that *value* and *goodness* are no more *characteristics* of things than is *being* or *existence*. We need not appeal to any "realm of eternal truths" in order to assure ourselves of the validity of our *a priori* knowledge. And we need not appeal to any

[6] [These have since been published as *Grundlegung und Aufbau der Ethik* (Bern: A. Francke, 1852), edited by Franziska Mayer-Hillebrand. R.M.C.].

"realm of eternal values" in order to safeguard the objectivity and absoluteness of our knowledge of value from subjectivism and relativism. Here we find the point at which many of our contemporary ontologists and Platonists have gone wrong. The metaphysical fictions in which they have lost themselves provide a welcome point of attack for contemporary positivists and relativists, and the result is a revival of the views of Protagoras. But Brentano finds the way between these two opposing views, and he is able to unify those points which each side holds, correctly, in opposition to the other. Thus, on the one hand, Protagoras and the subjectivists are right in holding that we must set out from the facts of consciousness and that we cannot speak meaningfully of value and of good without making reference to an evaluating subject. And, on the other hand, Plato and his present-day followers are right in insisting upon the absolute and universal validity of value. In order for a thing to be correctly preferred as being good or valuable, it is not necessary that that thing exist or even that there be anyone who evaluates it. What is needed is only this: that no evaluation of the thing can be experienced as being correct unless it is positive—unless it is one of love.

Although this work is not intended to present a system of ethics, it does attempt to indicate the relations that hold between the axioms of value and preference, on the one hand, and the derivative and therefore relative rules of practical morality, on the other. If the demands of society and the state are anything more than oppressive threats, then they must be related, in the way here indicated, to the principles of correct emotion. There could be no duty or obligation, other than mere external compulsion, unless the existence of certain ways of acting is to be preferred in itself to their non-existence.

Power and authority can oblige its subjects only to the extent that the exercise of such power is itself morally right. Demands may be justified, moreover, when there is no power or authority to assure their realization: for example, the requirements of so-called international law. Jurisprudence has no ethical or intellectual sanction once it is severed from the source that sustains it—the right and the just, recognized by emotions that are experienced as being correct. So, too, for economics, considered as a practical discipline. And "the theory of value" is itself without value unless it is based upon a theory of correct evaluation and preference. Political science and political economy would be vain delusions if, as some "political scientists" proclaim, all value judgements are beyond the sphere of science and knowledge. The latter opinion is now common, partly as a result of the decay of philosophy and partly as a result of a positivistic and historical orientation in science that has been nurtured by the imperialism of Roman law. But it is imperative that this view be eradicated. For the first condition for the intelligent regulation of social and international life is a common ethical consciousness, a unified fund of knowledge about the highest aims of mankind.

Socrates and Plato were mistaken in thinking that the mere knowledge of what is ethically right would be a sufficient condition for willing what is right. Such knowledge, nevertheless, is a *necessary* condition for willing what is right.

Knowing that there is a right and a wrong in the sphere of the emotions, we are able to see our way clearly in the dispute about determinism. The question of whether everything happens necessarily is independent of the question of whether there are valid ethical principles. In the case of judgement, no one needs to know whether or not a given judgement has a cause, or whether or not it was made necessarily, in order to be able to decide whether it is correct or incorrect. The correctness or incorrectness of an act of will is equally independent of the question of whether or not it has a cause. The sole justification for praise and blame, reward and punishment, lies in their social utility. Some have misunderstood Brentano's views on this point. We do not give equal praise to all correct decisions of the will. We give greater praise to those which have been preceded by internal struggle, for they are the decisions that require the greater encouragement.

The theory of ethical knowledge, as Brentano has developed it, is completely sovereign. The basis of obligation does not lie in the commands of any will—neither in one's own will nor in that of another, neither in a will that is human nor in one that is divine. It lies in one's own certain consciousness of the correctness of love and of hate. Thus we might say that ethics is neither heteronomous nor strictly autonomous; it is orthonomous. The principles of ethics are independent of the principles of metaphysics.

Yet it is only on the basis of metaphysics that we can decide the question between optimism and pessimism. Our consciousness makes clear to us that certain things are good and that some things are better than other things, and it sets up "the best of what is attainable" as the norm for all our actions. But the question whether more good than evil is in fact attainable is a question of metaphysics. Is that necessity which governs all things blind, or does it rule with insight and on the basis of emotional perfection? Ultimately, it is upon the answer to this question that the affirmation or negation of life—the preference between being and non-being—must depend. For those who are concerned about this question, I have included in the present edition of this work a number of brief selections in which Brentano sets forth his own answer.[7]

[7] For a more detailed and systematic statement, see Brentano's *Vom Dasein Gottes* (Leipzig: Felix Meiner, 1929), ed. Alfred Kastil, and his *Religion und Philosophie* (Bern: Francke Verlag, 1954), ed. Franziska Mayer-Hillebrand.

# Index

accidents, 137–40
*actus elicitus voluntatis*, 34
*actus imperatus voluntatis*, 34
Anaxagoras, 123
anger, 152–4
*a priori* knowledge, 14, 38, 111–13, 164
Aquinas, St. Thomas, 39, 42, 84, 87, 116
Aristotle, 5, 12, 13, 22–4, 29–30, 36, 39, 40–1, 44, 54, 56, 70, 73, 80–1, 87–90, 123, 148–9, 155, 160
atheism, 123–4
Augustine, St., 44

Bain, Alexander, 38, 39
being
  concept of being and existence, 57, 60–4, 73–5, 164
  in the sense of the true, 57–8, 63, 73
  *see also* truth
Benedict XV, 124
Beneke, F. E., 37, 84
Bentham, J., 30, 34, 36, 39
better, *see* preference
*bonum progressionis*, 115
Bossuet, Bishop, 86

categorical imperative, 37, 49–50
Catiline, 44
causation, 13, 81–2, 128–9
choice, 113–16, 151–2; *see also* preference

Christianity, 41–2, 117–18, 124
Cicero, 6–7
commands, 8–10, 37, 49–50, 92–3, 115–16
compensation, law of, 115
Comte, August, 95

Descartes, x, 15–17, 25, 50–4, 77, 83, 89–90, 123
descriptive psychology, ix, 11–16, 56
decision, *see* choice; preference
displeasure, *see* pleasure and displeasure

egoism, 40, 42
emotions, *see* anger; love and hate; pleasure and displeasure; preference
empirical knowledge, 13–14, 111–13
Epicurus, 28, 39, 40, 124
eudaemonism, 40
evident, the, 19–20, 43, 51, 76–83, 96–8, 163
existence, *see* being; truth

Fechner, G. T., 31, 40
Fenelon, F., 86
Francis of Assisi, St., 160
Franklin, Benjamin, 124, 125–9

Gauss, K. F., 3
God, 130–4, 158–9; *see also* theodicy
Goethe, 93

# INDEX

good
  concept of, 12–18, 75–6, 148–50
  highest practical, 32–7, 92–3, 95,
    127–30
  knowledge of, 18–24, 89–90, 111–
    113, 137
Grote, John, 8

Haneberg, Bishop, 93
happiness and unhappiness, 40, 134–7
Hartmann, Nicolai, 161
hate, see love and hate
Hegel, G. W. F., 37–8, 79
Helmoltz, H., 15, 41, 124
Heraclitus, 34, 135, 137
Herbart, J. F., ix, x, 10–11, 24, 57,
  93–4, 157–8
Herzen, A., 37
Holcot, Robert, 42
Horace, 92
Hume, David, 10, 21, 44, 76–7, 84,
  96–8, 158
Husserl, E., 161
Hye, Baron von, ix

ideas, 13–17, 141–2
Ihering, Rudolf von, 4–6, 12, 35–6,
  84, 93–6
indifferent, the, 26, 85
induction, 13, 24, 96–7, 113
innate concepts and principles, 4, 5,
  13–14

Jesus, 41
Jevons, S., 97
judgement
  apodictic, 82, 111–13, 147
  assertoric, 15–18, 54–9, 98–108,
    141–2
  double, 58–9, 107
  existential, 58, 60–73, 106–7
  negative, 64–73
  see also evident, the; ideas

Kant, I., 11, 37–8, 49–50, 75, 123
Kelvin, Lord, 124

Land, J. P. N., 59

Lange, Alfred, 38–9, 123
Laplace, Pierre Simon, 36
Leibniz, G. W., 3, 40, 45, 87, 115,
  123, 163
Leopardi, 160
Lessing, G. E., 41
Liebig, Justus von, 124
Locke, John, 5, 40, 123
logic, laws of, 9–10, 19–20, 38–9,
  81–2, 111–14
love and hate
  concept of, 16–21, 137–60
  correctness of, 17–24, 163–4
  objects of, 144–5, 150–1
  see also good; pleasure and dis-
    pleasure; preference; will, the

malum regressus, 115
Marty, Anton, 27, 59, 66, 115
Maxwell, J. C., 124
measurement in psychology, 30–1
Meinong, Alexius, 83, 161
Miklosich, Franz, ix, 16, 59–60, 98–
  108
Mill, James, 8, 97
Mill, John Stuart, 7–8, 12, 56, 83, 87,
  93, 96–8, 107
Möhler, Johann Adam, 42
Moore, G. E., 161–2
Müller, Johannes, 124

natural
  meaning of, 4
  sanction of law and morality, 4–34
necessity, 13–14, 111–13
Newman, J. H., 57
nominalists, 42

pacifism, 122–4
Pascal, B., 83, 157–9
perception
  external, 19, 21
  inner, 13–14, 138–40
Pflüger, Eduard, 124
Plato, 29–30, 36, 38–9, 45, 87, 123, 162
pleasure and displeasure
  concept of, 16–17, 20, 90–2, 148–
    157

pleasure and displeasure—*cont.*
  in the bad, 23, 90–1
  in the good, 23, 90–1
  natural, 148–9, 160
  sensuous and nonsensuous, 91–2,
    132–3, 155
preference
  concept of, 25–6, 127–8, 143–4
  correctness of, 26–9, 144
  rules of, 27–33
primary and secondary objects of
  consciousness, 139, 155
probability, 13, 96–7
Protagoras, 85, 88, 146, 162–3
'psychologism,' 80
punishment, 118–22

relativism in ethics, 35–6, 149
relativity of secondary moral laws,
  116–18
rigorism in ethics, 92–3
Rokitansky, Karl von, 5

Scheler, Max, 161
Schwann, Theodor, 124
Scotus, Duns, 39
Sigwart, C., 55, 60–73, 78–83, 85,
  87
Socrates, 34
sorites, 105

Spencer, Herbert, 97
Spinoza, 54
Steinthal, H., 59–60
Stoics, 39–40
Suarez, 54
subjectivism, 84–90, 92, 146, 157
subjectless propositions, 98–108
substance, 137–40
summation, rule of, 28, 40–1
synsemantic terms, 75–6, 164

theodicy, 24, 40, 115, 125–9, 130–4,
  167
Theresa, St., 86
time, 139
Trendelenberg, Adolph, 40, 79
truth, 14, 18, 57–61, 73, 73–5, 163

Uberweg, Friedrich, 84
Ulpian, 7
utilitarianism, 33, 35
ultimate ends, 12, 32, 95
"unconscious, the", 38

Wagner, S. Rudolf, 31
will, the
  antecedent and consequent, 114
  concept of, 11, 13, 50–4
  types of act, 34
Windelband, W., 51, 54–9, 75